PRIEST, PROPHET, KING

STUDY GUIDE

A Catholic Study Program presented by
MOST REV. ROBERT E. BARRON

Study Guide written by
CARL E. OLSON

www.WORDONFIRE.org

PRIEST, PROPHET, KING

Dear Friends in Christ,

The *Priest, Prophet, King* Formation Program has been created by Word on Fire Catholic Ministries to support the Church's mission, which is to introduce the world to Jesus Christ and invite people to share the many gifts the Lord offers and wants his people to enjoy.

We cannot introduce Jesus Christ to others unless we have first been introduced to him ourselves, and this is our purpose with the *Priest, Prophet, King* Formation Program—to provide an introduction to the Lord so that in coming to know him, people might better introduce him to others.

Jesus Christ is a living, divine person who, as the Scriptures testify, accepted a human nature and lived a real human life. This extraordinary revelation offers humanity new hope, for God in Christ shows us through his willingness to accept a human nature just how much he loves us. Christ the Lord in his revelation defines who he is. His truth is not simply a matter of an abstraction of the mind or feeling in our hearts. Instead, Christ is boldly himself, for he is God, but he is God who makes himself known to us and therefore gives us categories and experiences through which we can come to an understanding of who he is and what he wants.

These categories of understanding and experiencing a relationship with him are Priest, Prophet, and King and through them we come to know the Lord. They also allow us to understand ourselves.

The film for the *Priest, Prophet, King* Formation Program was created on location at the beautiful campus of Mundelein Seminary and the study program was written by my good friend, Carl Olson—it is my hope that the visual component of the Formation Program will inspire you with the beauty of the Lord and the written materials will provoke you to better appreciate his truth. I believe that in its totality, the *Priest, Prophet, King* Formation Program will help you know Christ and prepare you to truly be his missionary disciple.

Peace,

+ Robert Barron

Bishop Robert Barron
Auxiliary Bishop, Archdiocese of Los Angeles
Founder of Word on Fire Catholic Ministries

PRIEST, PROPHET, KING

PRIEST, PROPHET, KING

LESSON ONE
ADORATIO

ADORATIO

LESSON ONE DVD OUTLINE

I.   INTRODUCTION

    A. Christianity is a relationship with Jesus Christ

    B. Jesus is understood through the lens of the Old Testament

    C. Jesus is called "the Christ," meaning "the Anointed One"

    D. In the Old Testament, "anointed ones" were priests, prophets, and kings

    E. Jesus is the definitive Priest, Prophet, and King

    F. Through Baptism, we participate in Christ and share in his offices of priest, prophet, and king

II.   FIRST OLD TESTAMENT PRIEST: ADAM

    A. Priests perform sacrifices that unite divinity and humanity

    B. Before the Fall, Adam was the first priest because he was united with God and walked in easy fellowship with him in the Garden of Eden

    C. Adoratio means "mouth to mouth" or being perfectly aligned with God in right worship

III.   RIGHT WORSHIP LEADS TO HARMONY

    A. A properly integrated self: creature worshipping creator

    B. Well-ordered family, city, culture, and cosmos

    C. Garden of Eden/Heavenly Jerusalem is the true "culture of life"

IV.   WRONG WORSHIP LEADS TO DISINTEGRATION

    A. Sin

    B. Lack of unity with God

V.   NO COMMUNION WITHOUT SACRIFICE

    A. Temple sacrifice

    B. Getting rightly aligned to God will hurt (sacrifice)

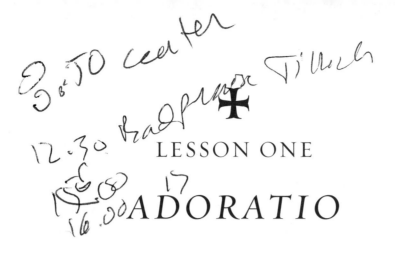

LESSON ONE

✠ ADORATIO

John the Baptist, having been arrested by Herod, sent some of his disciples to Jesus. Upon finding him, they asked the question that was on the minds of so many: "Are you the one who is to come, or are we to wait for another?" (Mt 11:2-3; Lk 7:19-20)

By this they meant, "Are you the Messiah, the Anointed One?" Some had wondered if John, the desert-dwelling preacher, might be the Messiah. He denied it directly: "I am not the Messiah" (Jn 1:20). But Jesus, of course, did not deny that he, the cousin of John, was the Messiah. Instead, he answered:

> "GO AND TELL JOHN WHAT YOU HEAR AND SEE: THE BLIND REGAIN THEIR SIGHT, THE LAME WALK, LEPERS ARE CLEANSED, THE DEAF HEAR, THE DEAD ARE RAISED, AND THE POOR HAVE THE GOOD NEWS PROCLAIMED TO THEM. AND BLESSED IS THE ONE WHO TAKES NO OFFENSE AT ME" (MT 11:4-6).

Later, at Caesarea Philippi, Jesus asked his disciples two questions, and they have resonated down through time ever since. First, he asked, "Who do people say that the Son of Man is?" The disciples responded, "Some say John the Baptist, others Elijah, still others Jeremiah or one of the prophets." In our own day, if the same question were asked, the response might be, "Some say a good teacher, others a wise guru, still others a life coach or one of the enlightened ones."

Then Jesus asked a second question: "But who do you say that I am?" Peter famously replied: "You are the Messiah, the Son of the living God" (Mt 16:13-16).

✠ THE MEANING OF MESSIAH

The title "Messiah," or "Christ" in Greek, is not just one of many names for Jesus, but a title of central importance. One bit of evidence for this can be found in the opening words of the Gospel of Matthew, written for Jewish readers: "The book of the genealogy of Jesus Christ, the son of

David, the son of Abraham..." (Mt 1:1). We are so accustomed to speaking of "Jesus Christ" that the boldness, the startling audacity, of those words can easily escape us. The Gospel of Mark, arguably the first of the four Gospels written, likewise commences with similarly surprising claims: "The beginning of the gospel of Jesus Christ, the Son of God" (Mk 1:1).

In both instances, there is a direct and intended allusion to the Old Testament (which, of course, was not "old" to either Mark or Matthew, but simply "Scripture"), and to the mysterious and oft-discussed Anointed One. Who was he? What would this "Christ" be like? What would he do? How would he reveal himself? Pope Benedict XVI, in homily given at a Chrism Mass at Saint Peter's (April 1, 2010), provided a helpful summary:

> "The word 'Christians,' in fact, by which Christ's disciples were known in the earliest days of Gentile Christianity, is derived from the word 'Christ' (Acts 11:20-21) – the Greek translation of the word 'Messiah,' which means 'anointed one'. To be a Christian is to come from Christ, to belong to Christ, to the anointed one of God, to whom God granted kingship and priesthood. It means belonging to him whom God himself anointed – not with material oil, but with the One whom the oil represents: with his Holy Spirit."

In the Old Testament, a priest was made so by anointing. Anointing was an act of consecration, of setting a man apart in a unique way for the word and work of God. But to be anointed was not just to be set apart. It was to be given the power and ability to perform the task given by God. Similarly, prophets and kings were declared so by anointing. The Anointed One—the One—would therefore be all three: priest, prophet, and king. "It was necessary that the Messiah be anointed by the Spirit of the Lord at once as king and priest, and also as prophet," explains the *Catechism of the Catholic Church*. "Jesus fulfilled the messianic hope of Israel in his threefold office of priest, prophet, and king" (par 436).

What is notable about the language of the Old Testament is that while priests, prophets, and kings were called "the Lord's Anointed" (1 Sam 24:6), "my Anointed" (1 Chron 16:22; Psa 105:15), or "his Anointed" (1 Sam 12:3-5;

Psa 18:50), there is no use of the term "Messiah." The Gospel writers and the other early Christians recognized and professed Jesus as Messiah, thus giving him a designation that is at once unique and yet also thoroughly rooted in the Jewish Scriptures. Michael F. Bird, in his study *Jesus Is the Christ* (InterVarsity Press, 2012), states:

> "The evangelists [Matthew, Mark, Luke, and John] clearly provide different appropriations of messianic traditions in their respective portrayals of Jesus, and the messiahship of Jesus functions differently in each Gospel. Yet there is a pervasive and shared conviction that Jesus is the Christos. The various titles assigned to Jesus (e.g. Son of God, Son of David, Son of Man) are expressions of the messianic role attributed to him. Also the citation, allusion, and echo of scriptural texts are built around the conviction that Jesus is the climax of Jewish scriptural expectations that point to the Messiah" (p 141).

For example, the Gospel of John describes how Andrew, one of disciples of John the Baptist, spent a day with Jesus and then searched out his brother, Simon, to say, "We have found the Messiah" (which means Christ)" (Jn 1:39-41). The same evangelist, John, in his first epistles declared, "Every one who believes that Jesus is the Christ is a child of God..." and "... we know that the Son of God has come and has given us understanding, to know him who is true; and we are in him who is true, in his Son Jesus Christ. This is the true God and eternal life" (1 Jn 5:1, 20). The messiah was always understood within the context of the reign or kingdom of God. And that, as we will see throughout this study, is at the heart of the person, teachings, and actions of Jesus, the Christ.

† PARTICIPATION IN CHRIST'S THREE-FOLD OFFICE

Jesus Christ, as Bishop Barron emphasizes, must be read and understood in light of the Old Testament "christs"—that is, those priests, prophets, and kings that foreshadowed the perfect Priest, Prophet, and King. In doing so, we not only deepen our understanding of the Messiah, we deepen our understanding of how each of us, as baptized Christians, participate in the life and work of Christ, sharing in his three-fold office of priest, prophet, and king.

Lumen Gentium, the Second Vatican Council's dogmatic constitution on the Church, begins by describing the grand vista of salvation history. God, in his wisdom and goodness, created all things, and his plan "was to raise men to a participation of the divine life" (2). The Son, Jesus Christ,

came to carry out the will of the Father, and so he "inaugurated the Kingdom of heaven on earth and revealed to us the mystery of that kingdom. By His obedience He brought about redemption. The Church, or, in other words, the kingdom of Christ now present in mystery, grows visibly through the power of God in the world" (3). *Lumen Gentium* explains in detail many aspects of the Church and the Kingdom, and how the two relate to one another. The Church, established by the new covenant, consists of both Jew and gentile, made into one people by baptism and the Holy Spirit—"new people of God." These people of God are, in the words of St. Peter, "a chosen race, a royal priesthood, a holy nation, a purchased people . . . who in times past were not a people, but are now the people of God" (LG 9; 1 Pet 2:9-10). These people, the conciliar fathers stated, are "messianic people" for Christ, the Messiah, is the head of the Church. And while this messianic people might "look like a small flock," they are being used by Christ "as an instrument for the redemption of all, and [are] sent forth into the whole world as the light of the world and the salt of the earth" (9). The document then emphasizes a key point: all of the faithful have been baptized, regenerated (that is, "born again"), and anointed by the Holy Spirit. And because of this, they "are consecrated as a spiritual house and a holy priesthood, in order that through all those works which are those of the Christian man they may offer spiritual sacrifices and proclaim the power of Him who has called them out of darkness into His marvelous light" (10).

Yes, there is an essential difference between the "common priesthood of the faithful" and "the ministerial or hierarchical priesthood." But the two are interrelated, and they each in their own way participate in the "one priesthood of Christ" (10). The ministerial priest has been ordained so that, acting in the person of Jesus Christ, he can make present the Eucharistic sacrifice, offering it to God "in the name of all the people." How do the non-ordained faithful share in the priesthood of Christ? First, by joining in the offering of the Eucharist. And:

> "They likewise exercise that priesthood in receiving the sacraments, in prayer and thanksgiving, in the witness of a holy life, and by self-denial and active charity" (10).

There is no competition between the common priesthood of all believers and the ministerial priesthood, for both rely completely on the singular priesthood of Jesus Christ, both are rooted in the life-giving sacrament of baptism, and both are at the service of the one, holy, Catholic, and apostolic Church. This means that every disciple of Jesus Christ—not just ordained priests or consecrated nuns—are to follow the exhortation of the Apostle Paul:

"I APPEAL TO YOU THEREFORE, BRETHREN, BY THE MERCIES OF GOD, TO PRESENT YOUR BODIES AS A LIVING SACRIFICE, HOLY AND ACCEPTABLE TO GOD, WHICH IS YOUR SPIRITUAL WORSHIP. DO NOT BE CONFORMED TO THIS WORLD BUT BE TRANSFORMED BY THE RENEWAL OF YOUR MIND, THAT YOU MAY PROVE WHAT IS THE WILL OF GOD, WHAT IS GOOD AND ACCEPTABLE AND PERFECT" (ROM 12:1-2).

This sharing of the laity in the three-fold office of Christ was of great importance to Saint John Paul II, who reiterated it throughout his pontificate. In fact, in the homily given on the inauguration of his pontificate on October 22, 1978, he stated:

"The Second Vatican Council has reminded us of the mystery of this power and of the fact that Christ's mission as Priest, Prophet-Teacher and King continues in the Church. Everyone, the whole People of God, shares in this threefold mission. Perhaps in the past, the tiara, this triple crown, was placed on the Pope's head in order to express by that symbol the Lord's plan for his Church, namely that all the hierarchical order of Christ's Church, all "sacred power" exercised in the Church, is nothing other than service, service with a single purpose: to ensure that the whole People of God shares in this threefold mission of Christ and always remains under the power of the Lord; a power that has its source not in the powers of this world but in the mystery of the Cross and Resurrection."

In his first encyclical, *Redemptor hominis* (March 4, 1979), John Paul II wrote that "the Church must be always aware of the dignity of the divine adoption received by man in Christ through the grace of the Holy Spirit and of his destination to grace and glory" (18). By having this clear and magnificent goal in view, the people of God are better suited for the service they are called to:

"The Church performs this ministry by sharing in the "triple office" belonging to her Master and Redeemer. This teaching, with its Biblical foundation, was brought fully to the fore by the Second Vatican Council, to the great advantage of the Church's life. For when we become aware that we share in Christ's triple mission, his triple office as priest, as prophet and as king, we also become more aware of what must receive service from the whole of the Church as the

society and community of the People of God on earth, and we likewise understand how each one of us must share in this mission and service" (18).

Finally, the *Catechism of the Catholic Church* teaches that the "whole People of God participates in these three offices of Christ and bears the responsibilities for mission and service that flow from them" (par 783). And:

> "On entering the People of God through faith and Baptism, one receives a share in this people's unique, priestly vocation: "Christ the Lord, high priest taken from among men, has made this new people 'a kingdom of priests to God, his Father.' The baptized, by regeneration and the anointing of the Holy Spirit, are consecrated to be a spiritual house and a holy priesthood" (par 784).

With that background in mind, let's look at the priesthood of Christ and how the faithful share in it.

† PRIESTHOOD

What does it mean to be a "priest"? Up until modern times, almost all cultures had some form of priesthood, and the role of priests was usually central to the culture of a particular people. The great British historian Christopher Dawson (1889-1970), in *Religion and Culture* (1948), explained:

> "Of all the social organs of religion the priesthood is that which has the most direct and enduring influence on culture. For priesthood represents religion embodied in a stable institution which forms an integral part of the structure of society and assumes a corporate responsibility for the religious life of the community."

While priests might also be teachers and educators, Dawson observed, "The primary function of the priest is not to teach. It is to offer sacrifice."

He then noted the assertion of St. Augustine that "there is no people without sacrifice." The act of sacrifice, as Dawson explains, "is the vital bond of communion between the people and its gods..." And the priest stands between the two, interceding in a unique way on behalf of the people.

Orthodox theologian and priest Fr. Alexander Schmemann (1921-83) made a similar but more theologically incisive observation in his classic book, *For the Life of the World* (1963). "The first and most basic definition of man is that he is a priest," wrote Schmemann. "He stands in the center of the world and unifies it in his act of blessing God, of both receiving the world from God and offering it to God—and by filling the world with this eucharist, he transforms his life, the one that he receives from the world." The sacrifice offered by man is, first and foremost, to offer proper praise and worship to God and to enter fully, in love, into communion with God. The power of man as priest, Schmemann explained in *Of Water and the Spirit* (1974), is fulfilled in sacrifice, which, "long before it became almost synonymous with 'expiation,' was and still is the essential expression of man's desire for communion with God, of creation's longing for its fulfillment in God, and which is essentially a movement, an act of praise, thanksgiving and union. Thus man is king and priest by nature and calling." The fall of Adam was due to his refusal to be priest. Rather than be filled and satisfied by God and his love, Adam chose to eat elsewhere, to seek satisfaction in something other than God. "The first consumer," argued Schmemann, "was Adam himself. He chose not to be a priest but to approach the world as consumer: to 'eat' of it, to use and to dominate it for himself, to benefit from it but not to offer, not to sacrifice, not to have it for God and in God."

Adam, as Bishop Barron explains, had perfect and intimate communion with God. He lived in God's love, breathing of God's divine life. Adam gave right worship and adoration—not because God needed it, of course, but because Adam needed it! For without true communion with God, man perishes—and true communion with God is established and nourished by loving and worshipping God. Adam, then, was a priest, and Eden was a perfectly ordered and life-affirming culture.

Understanding the nature of priesthood is foundational because it precedes the offices of king and prophet. It is, so to speak, primordial, for it situates the face-to-face, eye-to-eye relationship between Creator and the creature. It gets at the very essence of God's relationship with man.

Fr. Albert Schlitzer, C.S.C., in *Redemptive Incarnation* (1956), reflected on how Christ's priesthood, even more than his kingship and prophetic office, demonstrates that "the office of Christ as Priest

most perfectly of all reveals Him as Mediator tying God to man and man to God. …":

> "In the name of mankind He worships God to the full measure in which God deserves to be worshipped. … As the new Head of the human race, the Second Adam, He gives mankind back to God. This recognition of God's supreme dominion, and the total yielding up of one's self to the Supreme Being consequent upon that recognition, are at the very core of religion."

The great Jesuit scholar Jean Cardinal Danielou (1905-74) insisted that "Christ's work may be considered first as priestly, the offering of the perfect sacrifice which truly glorifies the Father, and which enables Creation to reach its goal" (*The Advent of Salvation,* 1950). Or, in the words of Danielou's friend, John Paul II:

> "In Christ, priesthood is linked with his Sacrifice, his self-giving to the Father; and, precisely because it is without limit, that self-giving gives rise in us human beings subject to numerous limitations to the need to turn to God in an ever more mature way and with a constant, ever more profound, conversion" (RH, 20).

The first Adam consumed the forbidden fruit, turning his back on the love of God; the second Adam consummated his life and divine mission by embracing the cross, revealing his perfect love for the Father and for the world. The first Adam's denial of love lead to death; the second Adam's denial of self opened the doors to life through death. "For as by a man came death," wrote St. Paul, "by a man has come also the resurrection of the dead. For as in Adam all die, so also in Christ shall all be made alive" (1 Cor 15:21-22).

The ministry of Christ—the Anointed One—was to proclaim glad tidings to the poor, grant liberty to captives, give sight to the blind, and free the oppressed. This is true restoration from the ancient exile of both Jews and Gentiles in the land of sin and darkness. Every man is invited by the

Messiah to leave the land of sin and enter the promised rest. "He set the captives free," wrote Cyril of Jerusalem, "having overthrown the tyrant Satan, he shed the divine and spiritual light on those whose heart was darkened."

Because of the Messiah's sacrifice, there is light and life. There is also a people—a messianic people who are also called to fellowship, sacrifice, and worship. Because of the Messiah's sacrifice, we can be priests again, able to love the world and to lead lives worthy of those called to be children of God. For, in the words of the conciliar fathers, "Christ, the final Adam, by the revelation of the mystery of the Father and His love, fully reveals man to man himself and makes his supreme calling clear" (*Gaudium et spes*, 22).

THEOLOGICAL REFLECTION:
VATICAN II & THE ROLE OF THE LAITY

For some Catholics, the Second Vatican Council was an updating of the Church that supposedly resulted in changes to the Church's goals and focus. This is, however, an unfortunate misreading. The Council was a renewal meant to aid Catholics in reappropriating and rediscovering the Church's goals and focus in a world that had changed dramatically in a short amount of time. The mission of the Church never changes, but our understanding of how to best live it in a specific culture does develop and change.

That mission, according to *Apostolicam Actuositatem*, the council's Decree on the Apostolate of Laity, is to proclaim the Gospel and to fill the temporal order with the light and salt of the Gospel; the laity have an essential role in this task:

"Christ's redemptive work, while essentially concerned with the salvation of men, includes also the renewal of the whole temporal order. Hence the mission of the Church is not only to bring the message and grace of Christ to men but also to penetrate and perfect the temporal order with the spirit of the Gospel. In fulfilling this mission of the Church, the Christian laity exercise their apostolate both in the Church and in the world, in both the spiritual and the temporal orders. These orders, although distinct, are so connected in the singular plan of God that He Himself intends to raise up the whole world again in Christ and to make it a new creation, initially on earth and completely on the last day. In both

orders the layman, being simultaneously a believer and a citizen, should be continuously led by the same Christian conscience" (AA 5).

It would be difficult to overstate the importance and centrality of the laity in this most pressing mission. According to *Lumen Gentium*, it is the laity's "special vocation . . . to seek the kingdom of God by engaging in temporal affairs and directing them according to God's will. . . . There they are called by God that, being led by the spirit to the Gospel, they may contribute to the sanctification of the world, as from within like leaven, by fulfilling their own particular duties. . . . It pertains to them in a special way so to illuminate and order all temporal things with which they are so closely associated that these may be effected and grow according to Christ and may be to the glory of the Creator and Redeemer" (LG 31).

The Council Fathers taught that "the laity must take up the renewal of the temporal order as their own special obligation," being led by the "light of the Gospel and the mind of the Church and motivated by Christian charity." This involves a permeation of culture, of society, and of all aspects of the kingdom of man with the "higher principles of the Christian life" (AA 7). John Paul II wrote that "in particular the lay faithful are called to restore to creation all its original value" (*Christifideles Laici*, 14). This task is not the priority of priests or religious; in fact, they are not qualified for, or capable of, such activity!

Only the laity, because of their skills in the marketplace, in the institutions of society, and in the everyday activities of men, can properly perform this crucial activity: "The apostolate in the social milieu, that is, the effort to infuse a Christian spirit into the mentality, customs, laws, and structures of the community in which one lives, is so much the duty and responsibility of the laity that it can never be performed properly by others" (AA 13). In other words, the laity need to realize they have important work to do, and the time to start that work is now.

Lesson One: QUESTIONS FOR UNDERSTANDING

Please use the commentary above and the references listed with each question to develop your answers.

1. What does the title "Messiah" mean? Although the term "Messiah" does not appear in the Old Testament, how is its use in the New Testament rooted in the Old Testament? (Mt. 16:13-20; CCC 436-40)

2. What are some passages from the Gospels and other New Testament books that identify Jesus as the Messiah? Why did the apostles and disciples think that Jesus was the Christ? (Mt. 1:1; 16:13-20; 26:63-4; Mk. 1:1; Lk. 4:41; Jn. 1:39-41; Acts 2:29-32; 1 Jn. 5:1, 20)

3. What does it mean to say that all of the baptized are priests? What distinguishes the ordained or ministerial priesthood from the common priesthood of all believers? (1 Pet 2:9-10; CCC 783-786)

4. What are essential features of priesthood? (Rom 12:1; CCC 1120, 1142, 1547)

5. Why is there such a close relationship in Scripture between love and sacrifice? What are some examples? (Mt 5:43-6; Jn 13:34-5; 15:12-17; Rom 12:1-2; Eph 5:1-2)

Lesson One: QUESTIONS FOR APPLICATION

1. How has your understanding of Jesus as Messiah changed or deepened?

2. What can you do to better offer yourself as a "spiritual sacrifice" to God?

3. How might you deepen and enrich your worship of God, both in private and in liturgy? How can you worship God in your daily thoughts, words, and deeds?

4. In what way are you a priest? What does that indicate about your relationship with Christ? With the Church? With your fellow Christians? With the world?

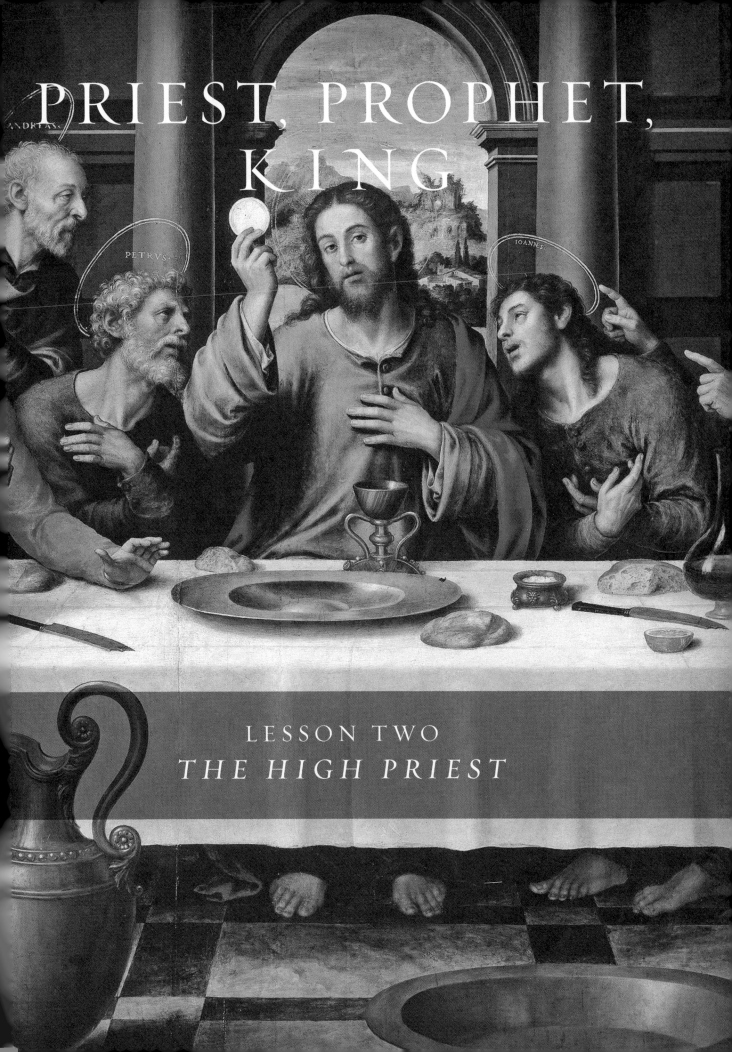

PRIEST, PROPHET, KING

LESSON TWO
THE HIGH PRIEST

THE HIGH PRIEST
LESSON TWO DVD OUTLINE

I.   JESUS IS THE FULFILLMENT OF THE PRIESTLY OFFICE
 A. Brings humanity and divinity together in one person
 B. Reconciles God and man

II. JOHN THE BAPTIST
 A. Interpretive lens to read Jesus
 B. Priestly family background
 C. Alternative temple in the desert
  1. Baptism with water
  2. Akin to temple's ritual cleaning from sin
 D. Identifies Jesus as the "Lamb of God," the consummate sacrifice

III. JESUS IS THE NEW TEMPLE
 A. Teaches
 B. Heals physically
 C. Forgives sins
 D. Replaces the temple in Jerusalem with the temple of his Body
  1. Sacrificed for our sins on the cross
  2. Eucharistic sacrifice of his body and blood

IV. JESUS IS THE DEFINITIVE TEMPLE, PRIEST, AND SACRIFICE
 A. Jesus bears all our sins just like the Old Testament scapegoat
 B. Jesus, as priest, is "mouth to mouth" with God while he is suffering on the cross
 C. Jesus' blood cleanses us from our sins once and for all, replacing all blood sacrifice of the old temple
 D. Water from Jesus' side symbolizes the restoration of the temple (Ezekiel prophecy)

V.   ALL THE BAPTIZED ARE CALLED TO RECONCILE GOD & HUMANITY
 A. Priestly responsibility
 B. Sustained by the Body and Blood of Christ in the Eucharist
 C. Called to bring about the Kingdom of God

Ex 37

23; 50
Corintless

✠

LESSON TWO

THE HIGH PRIEST

As we've seen, a deeply biblical understanding of priesthood and sacrifice does not begin with the Aaronic or Levitical priesthood, but goes back much further, to the very beginning, to the first chapters of Genesis. Adam was called to be a priest, which meant, among other things, that his fall was due to his failure to rightly exercise his priesthood. Instead of being satisfied by God and filled with divine love, Adam decided to find nourishment and fulfillment elsewhere, to be satisfied with something other than God.

To be a true priest requires obedience to the will and directive of God—being satisfied with God, who alone can truly satisfy. That obedience requires humility, while humility requires realism about who we are before God. Pride is indeed the opposite of humility, but that pride, at the root, comes from a failure to give proper worship, praise, and love to God. The noted speaker and theologian Frank Sheed, in *Genesis Regained* (Sheed & Ward, 1969), wrote:

> "To summarize: the one thing Genesis tells us of the sin is that it was an action of disobedience to God. There is no great point in speculating as to what the action was. The writer did not know; or regard it as important to know. He was not thinking in those terms. He was concerned with the choice of what one wants as against what God wants, the thrust of man's will against God's" (p. 103).

Scripture and patristics scholar Fr. Jean Daniélou, SJ articulated the same point in a slightly different manner, explaining that original sin "is the temptation for man to seize divine power by his own strength, and thus accomplish his salvation alone. It is the refusal to accept from God his salvation as a free gift" (*In the Beginning ... Genesis I-III* [Helicon, 1965], 55).

† SACRIFICE

True priesthood, then, demands sacrifice at every level. It is the sacrifice of illusions about one's powers and assumptions about one's abilities, especially when it comes to salvation from sin and

death. More positively, true priesthood reconciles the human and the divine; it brings together what was broken by a failure to give, to love, and to adore. In a very real way, it is about justice, for justice is ultimately what is due to someone. And what is due to God? Everything! How, then, in the Old Testament, could such an absolute and overwhelming fact be expressed? By sacrifice, especially the sacrifice of life and of things so necessary for life.

Msgr. Romano Guardini, in his classic book *The Lord* (Regnery Gateway, 1954, 1988), reflected on this fact in light of the sacrifice of Christ. The idea of sacrifice, he noted, is found everywhere in the Old Testament; its significance cannot be overstated (in fact, it is often understated). It is found in the story of Cain and Abel, in the account of Noah's thanksgiving after the flood, and in the narratives of the covenant established with Abram. "The whole order of religious life was regulated by sacrifice," wrote Guardini. "It ran like a crimson thread through Hebrew history, both in its national totality and in the history of the individual." He then asks, "What is sacrifice?"

> "It is man's offering of something which belongs to him, something precious and without flaw. This he gives away; gives to God, to keep. To express the completeness of God's ownership and the cancellation of man's, the gift is destroyed: the beverage which man himself could have drunk is poured on the ground; the first fruits of his harvest are burned; the animal is slain, consumed by fire and thus transported to its Creator."

Does God *need* such sacrifices? No, of course not. "In the eyes of God the gift in itself is nothing," Guardini observes:

> "But the intention behind it? This inspired by a sentiment of adoration, of thanksgiving, supplication, contrition or praise. The act of sacrifice is a concrete expression of man's recognized insignificance and his will to renunciation before the all-creative, omnipotent God who is the beginning and end of all things. It is a statement about who God is" (pp. 462, 463).

In the words of those assembled in the heavenly throne room, as described by John the Revelator: "To him who sits upon the throne and to the Lamb be blessing and honor and glory and might for ever and ever!" (Rev. 5:13) There is, however, another aspect of sacrifice, and it is vital to appreciating the singular and definitive priesthood of Jesus Christ: sacrifice is, as Guardini notes, "a passing over to God. In its deepest sense, to sacrifice means to enter into the life of God by renouncing the life of this world" (463). And thus, again, we see that sacrifice and priesthood are about the union and communion of God and man, divine and human, Creator and creature.

"What was the covenant but the attempt to bring the divine and human wills together?" asks Bishop Barron. "Who were the prophets but those who were calling people back to the Covenant? The whole Old Testament is about reconciling divinity and humanity." This essential point is often missed. Many Christians, it seems, think the Old Testament is about God's tireless search for revenge, retribution, and terrifying judgment. But the anger of God—in both the Old and New Testaments—is always directed against that which separates man from God: pride, lust, selfishness, idolatry, and so many other sins. God's passion is that of a lover hurt by seeing the one he loves destroying herself, watching the people he chose defiling themselves, seeing the world he created collapse upon itself in selfish ruin. He seeks us out so that we can discover and become what we are meant to be. God's search for man would result in God becoming man:

> "For Adam, the first man, was a figure of Him Who was to come, namely Christ the Lord. Christ, the final Adam, by the revelation of the mystery of the Father and His love, fully reveals man to man himself and makes his supreme calling clear" (*Gaudium et spes*, 22).

And that supreme call was first announced from the wilderness.

† JOHN THE BAPTIST AND THE "LAMB OF GOD"

"Repent, for the kingdom of heaven is at hand" (Mt. 3:2). John the Baptist, like all of the Old Testament prophets, issued a call to repentance, a return to the law, and a renewed commitment to the covenantal life instituted by Moses and David. The prophets were consumed by the call to conversion, and the greatest of the prophets was the cousin of Jesus: "Truly I say to you, among those born of women there has not arisen anyone greater than John the Baptist!" (Mt. 11:11) John, therefore, is not just a figure of passing interest, but is, as Bishop Barron notes, "a kind of interpretative lens through which we properly read Jesus." Fr. Hans Urs von Balthasar said that

two great saints—John the Baptist and the Blessed Virgin Mary—stand on either side of the gate into Advent, and they both "ask us why and with what intentions we are seeking admission" (*You Crown the Year with your Goodness* [Ignatius Press, 1989], pp. 251-2). Put another way, we cannot really know Jesus unless we meet and know the mother of Jesus and the forerunner of Jesus. Mary, of course, is the mother of Jesus—and thus the *Theotokos*, the Mother of God—through whom the Incarnate Word enters the world. And John is the voice in the wilderness who announces the public ministry and mission of the Incarnate Word.

"John surpasses all the prophets," remarks the Catechism, "of whom he is the last. He inaugurates the Gospel, already from his mother's womb welcomes the coming of Christ, and rejoices in being 'the friend of the bridegroom,' whom he points out as 'the Lamb of God, who takes away the sin of the world'" (CCC 523). But as the *Catechism* also points out, John was more than a prophet (CCC 719). He was also a priestly figure. His father, Zechariah, was a priest in the Temple in Jerusalem; his mother, Elizabeth, was from a priestly family; and he certainly must have been well acquainted with the temple practices, feasts, and liturgies. However, John's ministry was not in the temple in Jerusalem, but in the desert—a sort of alternative temple, free of the corruption and compromise that had become commonplace in Jerusalem:

> "IN THOSE DAYS CAME JOHN THE BAPTIST, PREACHING IN THE WILDERNESS OF JUDEA, 'REPENT, FOR THE KINGDOM OF HEAVEN IS AT HAND.' FOR THIS IS HE WHO WAS SPOKEN OF BY THE PROPHET ISAIAH WHEN HE SAID, 'THE VOICE OF ONE CRYING IN THE WILDERNESS: PREPARE THE WAY OF THE LORD, MAKE HIS PATHS STRAIGHT.' NOW JOHN WORE A GARMENT OF CAMEL'S HAIR, AND A LEATHER GIRDLE AROUND HIS WAIST; AND HIS FOOD WAS LOCUSTS AND WILD HONEY. THEN WENT OUT TO HIM JERUSALEM AND ALL JUDEA AND ALL THE REGION ABOUT THE JORDAN, AND THEY WERE BAPTIZED BY HIM IN THE RIVER JORDAN, CONFESSING THEIR SINS" (Mt. 3:1-6).

John, like the prophets Elijah and Elisha, lived in the wild, divinely chosen to be a lone voice in the wilderness. That wilderness is, first, the rugged and desolate land in which he dwelt. But the wilderness is also the world at large and throughout history. It includes the world today, which is a jungle of despair and trials, overgrown with temptations and filled with sins and evils of every sort. John was a stark and startling figure, but also one of obvious charisma and power. The Pharisees in Jerusalem were certainly curious, even concerned, and so sent priests and Levites to ask John, "Who are you?" He insisted, "I am not the Christ"; he also told them he was not Elijah.

> "They said to him then, 'Who are you? Let us have an answer for those who sent us. What do you say about yourself?' He said, 'I am the voice of one crying in the wilderness, 'Make straight the way of the Lord,' as the prophet Isaiah said'" (Jn. 1:19-23).

Yes, John was baptizing, but with water. The One he was announcing, John said, will "baptize you with the Holy Spirit and with fire" (Lk. 3:16). While "John's baptism was for repentance," says the *Catechism*, "baptism in water and the Spirit will be a new birth" (CCC 720). [All of John's actions and words focus like a laser on purity and holiness, on recognizing one's sin and being ready for the Holy One.] "The next day," the Fourth Gospel recounts, "he saw Jesus coming toward him, and said, 'Behold, the Lamb of God, who takes away the sin of the world!'" (Jn. 1:29)

And the next day, while with two of his disciples, John "looked at Jesus as he walked, and said, 'Behold, the Lamb of God!'" (Jn. 1:36) What did he mean? How was Jesus "the Lamb of God"? The most simple answer is that Jesus was a man prepared to be sacrificed, to be completely given over to God for the sake of world. God so loved the world that he gave his Son, and the Son so loved the Father, he gave himself for the world. To better appreciate this, we should be mindful of how the Gospel of John indicates in many places that Jesus is simultaneously the perfect sacrifice (the Lamb of God) and the new Temple (where God dwells and sacrifice takes place).

† SOMETHING GREATER THAN THE TEMPLE

Prior to the Baptizer's announcement, the Gospel states, "And the Word became flesh and dwelt among us, full of grace and truth; we have beheld his glory, glory as of the only Son from the Father" (Jn 1:14). This "glory" is a reference to the shekhinah glory of God, the divine presence and dwelling of God among his people. It manifested at Mount Sinai (Ex. 24:15-17), in the cloud that accompanied the tabernacle during the Exodus (Ex. 40:34-35), and in the cloud that filled the temple when Solomon finished building it:

> "When Solomon had ended his prayer, fire came down from heaven and consumed the burnt offering and the sacrifices, and the glory of the Lord filled the temple.

What did Solomon and the people do after God's glory filled the Temple? "Then the king and all the people offered sacrifice before the LORD" (2 Chron. 7:4). This is a simple but supernatural pattern. Jesus, the Lamb of God, came into the world and dwelt among us—and then gave himself as a sacrifice for the sins and the sake of the world.

Because he was fully God and fully man, Jesus alone could say, "I tell you, something greater than the temple is here" (Mt. 12:6). The stunning nature of this declaration—something greater than the temple—should not be missed. As Dr. Brant Pitre has shown in his essay "Jesus, the New Temple, and the New Priesthood" (*Temple and Contemplation: God's Presence in the Cosmos, Church, and Human Heart* [Letter & Spirit 4, 2008], 47-83), the temple was four key things for a devout first-century Jew: "(1) the dwelling-place of God on earth; (2) a microcosm of heaven and earth; (3) the sole place of sacrificial worship; (4) the place of the sacrificial priesthood." As Pitre explains, Jesus saw all four aspects of the temple being fulfilled in his person and actions, as well as in his disciples:

> "Indeed, the evidence in the Gospels strongly suggests that Jesus saw his own body as (1) the dwelling-place of God on earth; (2) the foundation stone that would be the beginning of a new Temple and a new creation; and (3) the sole place of sacrificial worship in the new covenant. Moreover, there are also good reasons to believe that he saw himself and his disciples as constituting (4) the new, eschatological priesthood that had been spoken of by the prophets" (p 48).

This is why Jesus, when being interrogated about his cleansing of the temple, said:

"'DESTROY THIS TEMPLE, AND IN THREE DAYS I WILL RAISE IT UP.' THE JEWS THEN SAID, 'IT HAS TAKEN FORTY-SIX YEARS TO BUILD THIS TEMPLE, AND WILL YOU RAISE IT UP IN THREE DAYS?' BUT HE SPOKE OF THE TEMPLE OF HIS BODY" (Jn. 2:19-21).

Jesus, then, presented himself as the perfect sacrifice, the new temple, and the final and unique high priest. Because he is sinless, he can be the Lamb of God without blemish. Because he is fully divine, he can be the temple, the dwelling place of God. Because he is fully man, he can be the everlasting high priest reconciling man to God, creation to Creator, sons and daughters to the merciful Father. All of this is also found in the book of Revelation, where Christ the Lamb is seen "standing, as if slain" (Rev. 5:6); he is worshipped (Rev. 5:8-12); he renders judgment upon mankind (Rev. 6:16); he saves his people (Rev. 7:9-17); he is the Bridegroom of the Church (Rev. 21:9); and he is the everlasting ruler (Rev. 22:3). And, yes, he is the new temple at the center of the New Jerusalem:

"AND I SAW NO TEMPLE IN THE CITY, FOR ITS TEMPLE IS THE LORD GOD THE ALMIGHTY AND THE LAMB. AND THE CITY HAS NO NEED OF SUN OR MOON TO SHINE UPON IT, FOR THE GLORY OF GOD IS ITS LIGHT, AND ITS LAMP IS THE LAMB" (Rev. 21:22-23).

† THE UNIQUE AND PERFECT HIGH PRIEST

As he approached the end of his earthly life, Jesus entered Jerusalem and ate a final meal, the Last Supper, with his disciples.

"NOW AS THEY WERE EATING, JESUS TOOK BREAD, AND BLESSED, AND BROKE IT, AND GAVE IT TO THE DISCIPLES AND SAID, 'TAKE, EAT; THIS IS MY BODY.' AND HE TOOK A CUP, AND WHEN HE HAD GIVEN THANKS HE GAVE IT TO THEM, SAYING, 'DRINK OF IT, ALL OF YOU; FOR THIS IS MY BLOOD OF THE COVENANT, WHICH IS POURED OUT FOR MANY FOR THE FORGIVENESS OF SINS'" (Mt. 26:26-28).

This is, as Bishop Barron highlights, the language of sacrifice. It refers back to the Mosaic covenant and accompanying sacrifices (Ex. 24:1-9); it certainly draws upon the sacrifices offered in the temple (2 Chron. 7:1). And it is squarely rooted in the Passover, when the suffering Hebrews were directed to take an unblemished one-year-old male lamb, kill it, and then smear the blood "on the two doorposts and the lintel of the houses in which they eat them" (Ex. 12:1-13). God told the people who were to be ready to leave Egypt: "The blood shall be a sign for you, upon the houses where you are; and when I see the blood, I will pass over you, and no plague shall fall upon you to destroy you, when I smite the land of Egypt" (Ex. 12:13).

There is another Old Testament connection, one of ancient and eternal importance. It is to a mysterious encounter and event that includes the first reference to a priest in sacred Scripture, taking place several centuries before the Hebrews had a priesthood:

"AND MELCHIZEDEK KING OF SALEM BROUGHT OUT BREAD AND WINE; HE WAS PRIEST OF GOD MOST HIGH. AND HE BLESSED HIM AND SAID, 'BLESSED BE ABRAM BY GOD MOST HIGH, MAKER OF HEAVEN AND EARTH; AND BLESSED BE GOD MOST HIGH, WHO HAS DELIVERED YOUR ENEMIES INTO YOUR HAND!' AND ABRAM GAVE HIM A TENTH OF EVERYTHING" (Gen. 14:18-20).

This is the only historical reference to Melchizedek in the Bible; the only other statement of his existence in the Old Testament is in Psalm 110, which is the most quoted Psalm in all of the New Testament: "You are a priest for ever after the order of Melchizedek" (Psa. 110:1-4). The other biblical references to the mysterious king and priest of Salem are found in the Epistle to the Hebrews, used by the author as evidence of the singular high priesthood of Jesus Christ: "We have this as a sure and steadfast anchor of the soul, a hope that enters into the inner shrine behind the curtain, where Jesus has gone as a forerunner on our behalf, having become a high priest for ever after the order of Melchizedek" (Heb. 6:19-20).

Who was Melchizedek? Why is he so significant? Needless to say, there has been much discussion about both questions by scholars and students of Scripture. First, the Canaanite roots of Melchizedek's name are fairly clear; it is commonly translated as *Milki* (my king) is *Zedek* ("righteousness" or "king of righteousness" [see Heb. 7:2]). It could be that "Melchizedek" is, in fact, more of a title than a proper name. There are several opinions as to Melchizedek's identity. One is that he was a Canaanite priest/king who ruled over the area of Jerusalem. Some have argued that he may have been Shem, the righteous son of Noah. Others hold that he is a mytho-poetic warrior who might have been an angel or archangel. Still others, including certain Jewish and Gnostic commentators, believed that Melchizedek was the Messiah. It seems that the first perspective, in general, is the best, even though additional details about Melchizedek aren't readily available.

The key point here is that the Epistle to the Hebrews is focused on the superior sonship and priesthood of Christ, and draws upon Psalms 2 and 110 in making its sophisticated theological case:

> "So also Christ did not exalt himself to be made a high priest, but was appointed by him who said to him, 'Thou art my Son, today I have begotten thee'; as he says also in another place, 'Thou art a priest for ever, after the order of Melchizedek.'

> In the days of his flesh, Jesus offered up prayers and supplications, with loud cries and tears, to him who was able to save him from death, and he was heard for his godly fear. Although he was a Son, he learned obedience through what he suffered; and being made perfect he became the source of eternal salvation to all who obey him, being designated by God a high priest after the order of Melchizedek" (Heb. 5:5-10).

All of Hebrews 7 continues to present this theological case, with several references to both Genesis 14 and Psalm 110. One point made by the author is that Melchizedek "is without father or mother or genealogy, and has neither beginning of days nor end of life, but resembling the Son of God he continues a priest for ever" (Heb. 7:3). The origin of this information is not evident, but the main point is clear: Jesus is superior to Abraham and the Jewish law, and his priesthood is superior to the Aaronic priesthood. Christ's priesthood does not rest on genealogies and it is not limited by temporal directives and cultic parameters, but is based in his divine sonship and his sacrificial death. As the the Epistle to the Hebrews argues throughout, Jesus is the high priest; he alone is able to offer a perfect, fitting, and eternal sacrifice, something the previous Jewish high priests could not do: "For it was fitting that we should have such a high priest, holy, blameless, unstained, separated from sinners, exalted above the heavens" (Heb. 7:26; see Heb. 8:1-7 and CCC 1544). It is important to note that all Catholic priests are such by virtue of their participation in the singular priesthood of Christ:

"The redemptive sacrifice of Christ is unique, accomplished once for all; yet it is made present in the Eucharistic sacrifice of the Church. The same is true of the one priesthood of Christ; it is made present through the ministerial priesthood without diminishing the uniqueness of Christ's priesthood: 'Only Christ is the true priest, the others being only his ministers'" (CCC 1545).

Melchizedek represents a time of purity, when the priesthood was not a caste system, but part of the natural order of family and tribal structure. With Christ, the requirements of priesthood have changed while also fulfilling the original vision intended for Adam, who was meant to have direct communion with God and to share in the divine life. That direct communion is now realized in and through Christ's perfect priesthood; we are welcome to participate in the Son's sacrifice and grow

in life through the reception of his priestly banquet, the Eucharist. As Daniélou wrote in another work, *The Bible and the Liturgy*:

> "There is, then, a greater resemblance to the Eucharist in the sacrifice of Melchizedek than in the Jewish sacrifices … It is the universal character of the sacrifice of the Eucharist which is signified by the appearances of bread and wine, and it is this that the liturgy of the Mass is stating when it shows us that it was prefigured in 'the holy sacrifice, the immaculate victim, offered by the high priest, Melchisedech'" ([University of Notre Dame Press, 1956], 146, 147).

Every time we come to Mass, as Bishop Barron reminds us, we are entering once more into the dynamic reality of Christ's cross, sacrifice, and gift of priesthood. Because of these gifts — and by God's grace — we are able to go into the world and work for the reconciliation of man with God, to heal divisions, and to bring people together. In a fallen world, filled with sin and division, there is no communion without sacrifice; there is no divine life without divine sacrifice. We have been washed in the blood of the Lamb (Rev. 7:14); we have been buried and united with Christ (Rom. 6). Through the power of the Holy Spirit, we now we go forth as living sacrifices (Rom. 12:1) to reconcile humanity to God, and to bring about his kingdom.

Please use the commentary above and the references listed with each question to develop your answers.

1. Why is the act of sacrifice so important in the Old Testament? What are some examples? (Gen 4:3-5 and 8:20-22; Exodus 24:3-8 and 40:16-30; 2 Chronicles 5:1-6 and 7:1-6; CCC 2580)

2. Why is John the Baptist so essential in the Gospels? What were his central messages? And what was his relationship with the temple? (Luke 1:5-17 and 3:1-18; CCC 523 and 719)

3. What did Jesus mean when he said, "I tell you, something greater than the temple is here" (Mt. 12:6)? How is Jesus the new temple? (John 1:14-18 and 2:19-21; Rev 21: 22-23; CCC 1197)

4. What is said about Melchizedek in the three places where he is mentioned in Scripture? How is he unique? What basic connection does the Epistle of Hebrews make between Melchizedek and Jesus? (Genesis 14:18-20; Psalm 110; Hebrews 7; CCC 1544)

Lesson Two: QUESTIONS FOR APPLICATION

1. How has your understanding of the nature of sacrifice deepened and changed? In what ways will that help you in your spiritual life and in your everyday life?

2. How might you gain a better appreciation for the person and mission of John the Baptist? If you were to pray to John the Baptist, what might you ask of him?

3. How can you more deeply contemplate the sacrificial nature of the Mass and the Eucharist? How can you give thanks to the Father for the gift of his Son? To the Son, for the gift of his life? To the Holy Spirit for the gift of divine life?

4. In what ways are you "the temple of the Holy Spirit"? How does that relate to Jesus Christ being the new temple?

PRIEST, PROPHET, KING

LESSON THREE
CHALLENGING
FALSE WORSHIP

LESSON THREE IMAGE

Christ Driving the Money Changers from the Temple. El Greco, 1600.

London. National Gallery.

CHALLENGING FALSE WORSHIP
LESSON THREE DVD OUTLINE

I.   A PROPHET SPEAKS THE DIVINE TRUTH
    A. As a "fool for Christ," sees the world differently than the rest of us
    B. Sees the world according to patterns of grace

II. ELIJAH IS THE OLD TESTAMENT MODEL OF THE PROPHET
    A. Sent by Yahweh to confront King Ahab for worshipping false gods
    B. Challenges the 450 priests of Baal who practice false worship that fails to prevail against the one, true God (1 Kings)
    C. Great demonstration of "right worship" or "worshipping the Creator and not the creature" or anything else

III. FALSE IDOLS OF TODAY (ST. THOMAS AQUINAS)
    A. Wealth
    B. Power
    C. Pleasure
    D. Honor

IV. DON'T SETTLE FOR ANYTHING LESS THAN GOD
    A. Fill your life with God, who is love and the sheer act of giving
    B. Don't strive to fill up your ego with wealth, pleasure, power, and honor as they will all disappoint you
    C. Surrender to God and make your life a gift

LESSON THREE

CHALLENGING FALSE WORSHIP

As Jesus went about his public ministry, interest and curiosity grew. Every miracle performed and each parable spoken resulted in larger crowds and increased scrutiny. Eventually, tensions arose with certain religious leaders and perplexed countrymen. The Evangelist Matthew recounts that Jesus, after an extended period of travel and teaching, came back "to his own country" and began to teach in the synagogue (Mt. 13:53-58).

The natural assumption is that Jesus would be welcomed with open arms, recognized for his astonishing miracles—such as casting out a demon from a blind and mute man (Mt. 12:22)—and his mesmerizing parables—of the sower and the seed, for instance (Mt. 13:1-23). Yes, the people were indeed astonished. But they were not welcoming. "Where did this man get this wisdom and these mighty works? Is not this the carpenter's son? Is not his mother called Mary? And are not his brothers James and Joseph and Simon and Judas? And are not all his sisters with us? Where then did this man get all this?" (Mt. 13:54-56)

Matthew provides a simple but profound description of this remarkable unbelief and distrust: "And they took offense at him." Jesus then says:

> "'A PROPHET IS NOT WITHOUT HONOR EXCEPT IN HIS OWN COUNTRY AND IN HIS OWN HOUSE.' AND HE DID NOT DO MANY MIGHTY WORKS THERE, BECAUSE OF THEIR UNBELIEF" (MT. 13:57-58).

Matthew then shifts the scene to John the Baptist, who had been imprisoned by the corrupt tyrant Herod the tetrarch. Herod wanted to execute John, but he was afraid to do so. Why? Because the people believed that John was a prophet (Mt. 14:1-5). John was eventually executed, of course, and his death hinted at what was to come for Jesus, who had earlier described his cousin John as both a prophet and "more than a prophet" (Mt. 11:7-11).

Fast forward to the end of Jesus' ministry. First, Jesus entered the city of Jerusalem on a donkey, an act that fulfilled "what was spoken by the prophet," a reference to two prophets: Isaiah and Zechariah (Mt. 21:4-5; see Isa. 62:11 and Zech. 9:9). Then Jesus went into the temple of God and drove out the money-changers, a prophetic action accompanied by another reference from Isaiah (Mt. 21:12-17; see Isa. 56:7). The next morning, he cursed the fig tree (Mt. 21:18-23), yet another prophetic act, this one meant to highlight the judgment of God and the lacking faith of Israel, both described centuries before by the prophet Hosea: "I found Israel like grapes in the wilderness; I saw your forefathers as the earliest fruit on the fig tree in its first season. But they came to Baal-peor and devoted themselves to shame, And they became as detestable as that which they loved" (Hos. 9:10). After entering the temple again, the chief priests and elders began to challenge and question his authority (Mt. 21:23-27).

Finally, Jesus delivered two more parables, and when the religious authorities heard them, "they perceived that he was speaking about them." Indeed he was! But like Herod, they were fearful, for the multitudes "held [Jesus] to be a prophet" (Mt. 21:45-46).

† PERCEIVING PROPHETIC STEREOTYPES

Those events described in the Gospel of Matthew provide a taste of the complicated and often contentious relationship between the biblical prophets and the Jewish leaders and people. "A prophet," wrote Archbishop Fulton Sheen, "is a Divine Troubler, not a political troubler. He is always a disturber of worldly peace; he makes listeners feel uneasy (*Those Mysterious Priests* [Doubleday, 1974], cited in *The Quotable Fulton Sheen* [Image, 1989], 251).

The Jewish rabbi and theologian Abraham J. Heschel (1907-72), in his two-volume work, *The Prophets* (Harper & Row, 1962), begins his introduction by stating: "This book is about some of the most disturbing people who have ever lived: the men whose inspiration brought the Bible into being—the men whose image is our refuge in distress, and whose voice and vision sustains our faith." Heschel then explained that the "significance of Israel's prophets lies not only in what they said but also in what they were. We cannot fully understand what they meant to say to us unless we have some degree of awareness of what happened to them" (ix). As true as that is about Isaiah, Amos, Hosea, Jeremiah, and the other prophets, it is even truer of Jesus, who is the fulfillment and perfect embodiment of the prophetic office.

As Bishop Barron states, the prophet is someone who is called by God to proclaim divine truth. The prophet has a unique relationship to words, especially to the words of God; the prophet is a proclaimer, called by God and gripped—sometimes against his natural instincts and desires—by the imperative to deliver the word entrusted to him. There is a deeply emotional quality to the prophetic office that is grounded in a profound love for both God and man, along with a passionate and righteous hatred for sin, idolatry, and injustice. "The prophet is a man who feels fiercely," wrote Heschel. "God has thrust a burden upon his soul, and he is bowed and stunned at man's fierce greed. … Prophecy is the voice that God has lent to the silent agony, a voice to the plundered poor, to the profaned riches of the world. It is a form of living, a crossing point of God and man (*The Prophets*, 5, 6).

Prophets are sometimes perceived as being cranky loners and half-crazed wild men who are outside of the normal life of the community and nation. There is an element of truth in that perception, but it misses how deeply focused the prophets were on the very heart of Israel as a chosen people, a heart located in the law and the covenant. The prophets cried out for a renunciation of sin and a return to holiness. The *Catechism* remarks:

> "Through the prophets, God forms his people in the hope of salvation, in the expectation of a new and everlasting Covenant intended for all, to be written on their hearts. The prophets proclaim a radical redemption of the People of God, purification from all their infidelities, a salvation which will include all the nations" (par. 64).

Prophets are also often depicted as being obsessed with foretelling the future and of delivering messages of woe and gloom and doom. Again, there is some truth in that portrait, for the prophets did speak often about the future, and their messages were often filled with dark warnings. But *foretelling* events taking place in the near future was most often a way of proving that what the prophet was *forth-telling* demanded close attention. It was, so to speak, proof of authenticity— quite understandable when there were often false prophets making false claims, usually at the behest of a false god. And foretelling events in the more distant future was always rooted in a deep understanding of the history of Israel, the law given to Israel, and the covenants established with Israel.

† PROPHECY, LAW, & COVENANT

This latter point is vital to understanding the Old Testament prophets and appreciating how Jesus fulfills the role of prophet through his words and deeds. The messages of the prophets were given in response to specific current events—acts of injustice, corruption in the temple or the court, idolatry, alliances with pagan rulers, and so forth—that are recorded in the historical books of Joshua, Judges, Ruth, Samuel, Kings, Chronicles, Ezra, Nehemiah, Tobit, Judith, Esther, and Maccabees. Those actions were evaluated by the prophets in the light of the law, and the accusations and condemnations uttered by the prophets were based in the covenant, especially in the blessings and curses outlined in Leviticus (especially chapter 26) and Deuteronomy (especially chapters 28-30, 32).

It is striking how so many of the prophetic predictions of national ruin, captivity, and exile flow from the curses expounded by the first great prophet, Moses, within the law, as a part of the covenantal relationship between God and the people. Here are two examples:

> "BUT IF YOU WILL NOT HEARKEN TO ME, AND WILL NOT DO ALL THESE COMMANDMENTS, IF YOU SPURN MY STATUTES, AND IF YOUR SOUL ABHORS MY ORDINANCES, SO THAT YOU WILL NOT DO ALL MY COMMANDMENTS, BUT BREAK MY COVENANT, I WILL DO THIS TO YOU: I WILL APPOINT OVER YOU SUDDEN TERROR, CONSUMPTION, AND FEVER THAT WILL WASTE THE EYES AND CAUSE LIFE TO PINE AWAY. AND YOU SHALL SOW YOUR SEED IN VAIN, FOR YOUR ENEMIES SHALL EAT IT; I WILL SET MY FACE AGAINST YOU, AND YOU SHALL BE SMITTEN BEFORE YOUR ENEMIES; THOSE WHO HATE YOU SHALL RULE OVER YOU, AND YOU SHALL FLEE WHEN NONE PURSUES YOU" (LEV. 26:14-17).

> "BUT IF YOU WILL NOT OBEY THE VOICE OF THE LORD YOUR GOD OR BE CAREFUL TO DO ALL HIS COMMANDMENTS AND HIS STATUTES WHICH I COMMAND YOU THIS DAY, THEN ALL THESE CURSES SHALL COME UPON YOU AND OVERTAKE YOU. ... THE LORD WILL CAUSE YOU TO BE DEFEATED BEFORE YOUR ENEMIES; YOU SHALL GO OUT ONE WAY AGAINST THEM, AND FLEE SEVEN WAYS BEFORE THEM; AND YOU SHALL BE A HOR-

ROR TO ALL THE KINGDOMS OF THE EARTH. … YOUR SONS AND YOUR DAUGHTERS SHALL BE GIVEN TO ANOTHER PEOPLE, WHILE YOUR EYES LOOK ON AND FAIL WITH LONGING FOR THEM ALL THE DAY; AND IT SHALL NOT BE IN THE POWER OF YOUR HAND TO PREVENT IT. A NATION WHICH YOU HAVE NOT KNOWN SHALL EAT UP THE FRUIT OF YOUR GROUND AND OF ALL YOUR LABORS; AND YOU SHALL BE ONLY OPPRESSED AND CRUSHED CONTINUALLY…" (DEUT. 28:15, 25, 32-33).

This helps us to better appreciate what Bishop Barron means when he says, "Prophets don't look at a different world than anyone else. A Jew, a Christian, a Hindu, a Muslim—we all see the same world. But prophets see it as *something*. They see it according to the patterns of grace." The law and the covenant established a pattern of right relationship and of holy living, and the prophets saw the past, the present, *and* the future, according to that pattern.

The British Old Testament scholar R. E. Clements, in *Prophecy and Covenant* (SCM Press, 1965, 1969), explains this relationship is detail. One of his basic arguments is that the prophets, although having different personalities and being in different situations, squarely based their prophetic work on the foundation of the law and covenant. "The institution of a tradition of law, with both ethical and cultic regulations, was indigenous to Israel's cult, and forms a permanent feature of the covenant relationship between Yahweh and Israel. It is to this tradition of a covenantal code of conduct that the great prophets of the eighth and seventh centuries [B.C.] appealed when they accused their nation of disloyalty to Yahweh, and of disregard of his revealed demands" (p. 23). He also emphasizes the historical vision implicit in the prophetic work:

> "The prophets were first and foremost interpreters of history, and in particular of the course of historical events which meant defeat, suffering and exile for the kingdoms of Israel and Judah, during the eighth, seventh and sixth centuries BC. The great political events which filled their horizons were fraught with significance for them because they were a part of Yahweh's dealings with Israel. By enabling Israel to understand its history in the light of its obligations to the covenant the prophets saved Israel from both arrogance and despair. … The awareness that the judgment had fallen, and that God in his mercy was calling them to a new beginning, was a primary datum of their faith. … It was by taking heed to the message of the prophets that Israel was, after the exile, able to find meaning in its experience and hope for its future."

This emphasis on prophecy being oriented toward God's mercy and mankind's hope is notable, especially since the "God of the Old Testament" (as some refer to him) is often, and quite

incorrectly, viewed as a God of vengeance, anger, and wrath. However, it is far better to see God as he presents himself:

"For I am the LORD your God; consecrate yourselves therefore, and be holy, for I am holy. ... For I am the LORD who brought you up out of the land of Egypt, to be your God; you shall therefore be holy, for I am holy" (Lev. 11:44-45).

God does not desire mankind's obedience for his own sake (since he lacks nothing), but for mankind's sake. And the prophets did not warn and exhort and criticize because they were angry, petty men, but because they loved God, God's law and covenant, and God's people. Put another way, judgment is always aimed at the destruction of what separates man from God: greed, injustice, fornication, idolatry, and so forth.

And the things that separate us from God are also substitutes for God. As Bishop Barron has explained, there are four great substitutes identified by the Angelic Doctor, St. Thomas Aquinas: wealth, pleasure, power, and honor. These four substitutes—or idols, in biblical terms—transcend cultural and chronological divides, as reading the Old Testament readily demonstrates. For example, the prophet Jeremiah, who prophesied for forty years during the reigns of three kings and into the fall of Jerusalem in 587 B.C., warned: "Your wealth and your treasures I will give as spoil, without price, for all your sins, throughout all your territory" (Jer. 15:13).

It was not a coincidence that the prophets became a recognized and distinct group of men about the same time that God allowed the people to choose an earthly king. They were, in a sense, a "check and balance" on the abuse of power that often occurred in the royal courts. One of the first was the prophet Nathan, who chastised King David for adultery and murder: "Why have you despised the word of the LORD, to do what is evil in his sight? ... Now therefore the sword shall never depart from your house, because you have despised me..." (2 Sam. 12:9-10). And the prophet Ezekiel, whose book is one of the most ferocious and beautiful in all of Scripture, railed against the sensuality of Judah and Jerusalem as the people languished in exile in Babylon:

"FOR THUS SAYS THE LORD GOD: BEHOLD, I WILL DELIVER YOU INTO THE HANDS OF THOSE WHOM YOU HATE, INTO THE HANDS OF THOSE FROM WHOM YOU TURNED IN DISGUST; AND THEY SHALL DEAL WITH YOU IN HATRED, AND TAKE AWAY ALL THE FRUIT OF YOUR LABOR, AND LEAVE YOU NAKED AND BARE, AND THE NAKEDNESS OF YOUR HARLOTRY SHALL BE UNCOVERED. YOUR LEWDNESS AND YOUR HARLOTRY HAVE BROUGHT THIS UPON YOU, BECAUSE YOU PLAYED THE HARLOT WITH THE NATIONS, AND POLLUTED YOURSELF WITH THEIR IDOLS" (EZEK. 23:28-30).

Again, all of these things are, in the end, idols. And if there is one thing the prophets despise and attack with relentless vigor it is each and every form of idolatry. Not because God is needy, or simply a moralist, but because he is holy and Other. He alone deserves our worship, our gifts, our entire being. God is a sheer act of giving who asks that we give completely in return. And how does he ask? Through words, of course. And then, later, through The Word, the Incarnate Son of God.

† PROPHETS & THE WORD OF GOD

It's impossible to overstate the importance of words—specifically, the word of God—in the life and work of the prophets. The Scripture scholar Fr. Michael Duggan, in *The Consuming Fire: A Christian Introduction to the Old Testament* (Ignatius Press, 1991), writes, "Prophecy is the discernment of God's action and the communication of his will at a specific point in history." He then offers a definition of the prophets that makes three points about the relationship between the prophets and God's word:

> "A prophet is a man or woman anointed by God and ultimately recognized by the people to announce God's word to his or her generation. The prophet is a servant of the word who receives revelation and personally experiences its power for judgment and salvation even as he or she proclaims it to others. Therefore, prophecy is an intensely personal event that begins in God and shapes the prophet's life to foreshadow the manner in which the prophetic word will form the community of God's people." (p. 235)

Put simply, the prophet is identified by three characteristics: he is chosen by God to announce God's word; he is an obedient servant of God's word; and he is shaped by God's word for the sake of God's people. Those basic truths are found in the writings and lives of Ezekiel and Amos, Malachi and Daniel, Jeremiah and Jonah, and all the rest of the prophets.

As we'll see in greater detail in the next study, Jesus perfectly exemplifies all of these attributes. Not only that, he calls every one of us, by virtue of our baptism and union with him, to do the same. This is why Saint John Paul II, in his post-synodal apostolic exhortation, *Christifideles Laici* ("*On the Vocation and Mission of the Lay Faithful in the Church*" [Dec. 30, 1988]), stated:

> "Through their participation in the prophetic mission of Christ, 'who proclaimed the kingdom of his Father by the testimony of his life and by the power of his world,' the lay faithful are given the ability and responsibility to accept the gospel in faith and to proclaim it in word and deed, without hesitating to courageously identify and denounce evil. United to Christ, the 'great prophet' (Lk 7:16), and in the Spirit made 'witnesses' of the Risen Christ, the lay faithful are made sharers in the appreciation of the Church's supernatural faith, that "cannot err in matters of belief" and sharers as well in the grace of the word (cf. Acts 2:17-18; Rev 19:10). They are also called to allow the newness and the power of the gospel to shine out everyday in their family and social life, as well as to express patiently and courageously in the contradictions of the present age their hope of future glory even 'through the framework of their secular life.'"

The three characteristics are readily evident: the laity are called to accept and then proclaim the Gospel. Why? Because they are witnesses of Jesus Christ and sharers in the Church's faith and the grace of the word. For what purpose? So that the power of the Gospel can shine forth, correcting errors and presenting the hope of future glory—that is, eternal life with God.

There are three qualities of the word of God, as expressed in Scripture, that might escape our notice since we can tend think of words in a rather abstract, detached sense. The word of God is personal, powerful, and performative. In other words, is intimate, it is life-changing, and it accomplishes what it seeks to accomplish. In fact, the three qualities are so deeply intertwined and perfectly unified that while they can be distinguished, they really cannot be separated. One of the earliest examples is found in the Pentateuch, not long after God had revealed himself in the burning bush as "I Am Who I Am" to Moses (Ex. 3:14). God called Moses to return to Egypt in order to deliver the Hebrews from four hundred years of slaver

But Moses was fearful; he also lamented his lack of eloquence: "I am slow of speech and of tongue" (Ex. 4:10). God replied: "Who has made man's mouth? Who makes him dumb, or deaf, or seeing, or blind? Is it not I, the LORD?" Moses persisted in his claim to being speech-challenged, and so God appointed Moses' brother, Aaron, to be a sort of prophetic instrument:

> "AND YOU SHALL SPEAK TO HIM AND PUT THE WORDS IN HIS MOUTH; AND I WILL BE WITH YOUR MOUTH AND WITH HIS MOUTH, AND WILL TEACH YOU WHAT YOU SHALL DO. HE SHALL SPEAK FOR YOU TO THE PEOPLE; AND HE SHALL BE A MOUTH FOR YOU, AND YOU SHALL BE TO HIM AS GOD" (EX. 4:15-16; SEE EX. 7:1-2).

However, it was Moses who would become known among the Israelites as one of the two greatest prophets, the other being Elijah (cf. The Transfiguration; Matt. 17:1-4). Eloquence was not an essential characteristic of the prophet; a true prophet was not a master speaker, but was a man directly chosen by God and given his divine word. The prophets, observed Fr. John L. McKenzie in *The Two-Edge Sword* (Image, 1966), "recommended themselves not for their learning, their experience, their wisdom, their power, but for this only, that the word of the Lord had come to them" (p. 45). The prophet had an intimate, direct, and unique relationship with God; like a priest, he acted as a sort of intermediary between God and the people:

> "AND THE LORD CAME DOWN UPON MOUNT SINAI, TO THE TOP OF THE MOUNTAIN; AND THE LORD CALLED MOSES TO THE TOP OF THE MOUNTAIN, AND MOSES WENT UP. AND THE LORD SAID TO MOSES, 'GO DOWN AND WARN THE PEOPLE, LEST THEY BREAK THROUGH TO THE LORD TO GAZE AND MANY OF THEM PERISH'" (EX. 19:20-21).

The intimacy and power of God's call and word is revealed dramatically in the experiences of Isaiah and Jeremiah. The former, having been given a startling vision of the heavenly throne room of God, exclaimed, "Woe is me! For I am lost; for I am a man of unclean lips, and I dwell in the midst of a people of unclean lips; for my eyes have seen the King, the LORD of hosts!" A seraphim then touched a burning coal from the heavenly altar to Isaiah's mouth, saying, "Behold, this has touched your lips; your guilt is taken away, and your sin forgiven" (Isa. 6:1-7).

The youthful Jeremiah had a similar experience, which he recounted in a matter-of-fact manner: "Now the word of the LORD came to me saying, 'Before I formed you in the womb I knew you, and before you were born I consecrated you; I appointed you a prophet to the nations.'" Jeremiah, like Moses, claimed to lack the ability to speak well, although he appealed, rather understandably, to his youthfulness:

"Then I said, 'Ah, Lord GOD! Behold, I do not know how to speak, for I am only a youth.' But the LORD said to me, 'Do not say, "I am only a youth"; for to all to whom I send you shall go, and whatever I command you shall speak. Be not afraid of them, for I am with you to deliver you, says the LORD.' Then the LORD put forth his hand and touched my mouth; and the LORD said to me, 'Behold, I have put my words in your mouth'" (Jer. 1:6-9).

That act—"and touched my mouth"—is personal, powerful, and performative. One of the most poetic descriptions of the power of God's word was given by Isaiah:

"For as the rain and the snow come down from heaven, and return not thither but water the earth, making it bring forth and sprout, giving seed to the sower and bread to the eater, so shall my word be that goes forth from my mouth; it shall not return to me empty, but it shall accomplish that which I purpose, and prosper in the thing for which I sent it" (Isa. 55:10-11).

The words of the prophets, as Bishop Barron notes, "are simultaneously rich, beautiful, and lyrical, but also unnerving and disturbing." The prophets, having been directly touched, transformed, and compelled by God's word, delivered that same challenging word to people who often ignored the prophets, and just as often mocked and attacked them. The Old Testament prophets were men possessed—by God, by God's word, by divine truth—but that did not guarantee an eager and humble audience. Quite the contrary! The prophets were feared and ill-treated; they were men without honor.

The Epistle to the Hebrews opens by stating: "In many and various ways God spoke of old to our fathers by the prophets; but in these last days he has spoken to us by a Son, whom he appointed the heir of all things, through whom also he created the world" (Heb. 1:1-2). God sent forth his Son, the Word, to accomplish what he purposed: the proclamation of the Kingdom, the redemption of the world, the salvation of man, the renewal of all things. In the next study, we will examine how Jesus is the Prophet *par excellence*, and how all those who share in his divine life are called to be prophets by virtue of their baptism.

Lesson Three: QUESTIONS FOR UNDERSTANDING

Please use the commentary above and the references listed with each question to develop your answers.

1. What are some of the distinguishing qualities of the Old Testament prophets? What is a one-sentence description of a biblical prophet?

2. Were the prophets primarily focused on foretelling the future? (CCC 64)

3. What was the relationship between the prophets, the law, and the Covenant? (Lev 26; Deut 28)

4. According to St. Thomas Aquinas, what are the four great substitutes for God? What examples of these can be given from stories in the Old Testament?

5. How would you describe the relationship between the prophets and the word of God? What are three essential qualities of the divine word?

Lesson Three: QUESTIONS FOR APPLICATION

1. Prior to this study, how did you think of the Old Testament prophets? How has your understanding of them changed?

2. How does your increased understanding of prophets help you better understand both the work and person of Jesus, as well as your vocation to be a prophet, rooted in the sacrament of baptism?

3. What messages of the prophets seem most needed in today's world? In your own life?

4. What quality of the Old Testament prophets do you most admire? How might you grow in that particular quality in your daily life?

5. How is the word of God personal, powerful, and performative in your life? What can you do to better recognize and appreciate the intimacy, power, and transforming nature of God's word?

6. How might you, as a lay person or priest or religious, be called to carry out your prophetic work in your home and in the outside world?

PRIEST, PROPHET, KING

LESSON FOUR
THE WORD MADE FLESH

THE WORD MADE FLESH
LESSON FOUR DVD OUTLINE

I.   JESUS IS THE DIVINE TRUTH IN PERSON

    A.   "In the beginning was the Word" or the divine pattern and the divine pattern became human flesh

    B.   Jesus kept his Messianic identity quiet, but accepted his prophetic identity by preaching the divine truth often

II. KEY PREACHING IS SERMON ON THE MOUNT

    A.   "Negative" Beatitudes: Avoiding False Worship

        1.   *"Blessed are the poor in spirit"*

            a.   Detached from wealth and material things

            b.   Focused on doing the will of God whether rich or poor

        2.   *"Blessed are those who mourn"*

            a.   Not attached or addicted to good feelings or making sensual pleasure your god

            b.   Focused on doing the will of God no matter how you feel

        3.   *"Blessed are the meek"*

            a.   Not attached or addicted to power

            b.   Focused on doing the will of God whether powerful or not

        4.   *"Blessed are you when people persecute you and hate you because of me"*

            a.   Not attached or addicted to the approval of others

            b.   Focused on doing the will of God no matter what others think

    B.   "Positive" Beatitudes: What happens when you are practicing right worship

        1.   *"Blessed are the merciful"*

        —When aligned with God, your are a vehicle for his mercy

        2.   *"Blessed are the pure of heart"*

        —Single-mindedly focused on God and what he wants

        3.   *"Blessed are you if you hunger and thirst for righteousness"*

        ——Righteousness is God's will, which you will seek if you are in right worship

4. *"Blessed are the peacemakers, for they shall be called children of God."*

   —The saints radiate peace

III. "LOVE WHAT JESUS LOVED ON THE CROSS AND DESPISE WHAT HE DESPISED ON THE CROSS"

   A. Jesus despised wealth, pleasure, power, and honor

   B. Jesus loved doing the will of his Father and was the ultimate peacemaker

IV. SEEK BIBLICAL FREEDOM

   A. Freedom from false gods

   B. Freedom from addictions

   C. Freedom from false worship

   D. Freedom to do the will of God

LESSON FOUR

THE WORD MADE FLESH

In the introduction to *Jesus of Nazareth: From the Baptism in the Jordan to the Transfiguration* (Doubleday, 2007), the first volume of his trilogy on the life and teachings of Christ, Pope Benedict XVI wrote:

"The Book of Deuteronomy contains a promise that is completely different from the messianic hope expressed in other books of the Old Testament, yet it is of decisive importance for understanding the figure of Jesus. The object of this promise is not a king of Israel and king of the world—a new David, in other words—but a new Moses. Moses, himself, is interpreted as a prophet." (p. 1)

Benedict then explains how the understanding of "prophet" found in the Old Testament is unique, being substantially different in nature from the prophets of "the surrounding religious world, something that Israel alone has in this particular form." That uniqueness was due to the nature of the true God and the relationship the people had with him through faith and covenant. Whereas pagan cultures had prophets and soothsayers who were fixated on divining the future and foretelling fortunes, the people of Israel were warned against the obsessive, even dangerous, nature of such practices. This is clear in the warning given to the people, through Moses:

"WHEN YOU COME INTO THE LAND WHICH THE LORD YOUR GOD GIVES YOU, YOU SHALL NOT LEARN TO FOLLOW THE ABOMINABLE PRACTICES OF THOSE NATIONS. THERE SHALL NOT BE FOUND AMONG YOU ANY ONE WHO BURNS HIS SON OR HIS DAUGHTER AS AN OFFERING, ANY ONE WHO PRACTICES DIVINATION, A SOOTHSAYER, OR AN AUGUR, OR A SORCERER, OR A CHARMER, OR A MEDIUM, OR A WIZARD, OR A NECROMANCER. FOR WHOEVER DOES THESE THINGS IS AN ABOMINATION TO THE LORD; AND BECAUSE OF THESE ABOMINABLE PRACTICES THE LORD YOUR GOD IS DRIVING THEM OUT BEFORE YOU" (DEUT. 18:9-12).

✝ THE FUTURE PROPHET

Trying to see into the "window" of the future, as Benedict describes it, is an "abomination" to God, for it is opposed to a life of holy and humble faith. And it was in this context that a most significant promise, often overlooked or ignored, was given:

> "THE LORD YOUR GOD WILL RAISE UP FOR YOU A PROPHET LIKE ME FROM AMONG YOU, FROM YOUR BRETHREN—HIM YOU SHALL HEED … AND I WILL PUT MY WORDS IN HIS MOUTH, AND HE SHALL SPEAK TO THEM ALL THAT I COMMAND HIM" (DEUT. 18:15, 18-19).

This mysterious promise—a prophesy of a future prophet by the prophet Moses—was followed by warnings against false prophets, who were to be tested and then dealt with firmly, even harshly (Deut. 18:18-20). There is then a long silence about this mysterious future prophet until the very end of Deuteronomy. There, in the concluding words of the Pentateuch, the prophet is mentioned again:

> "AND THERE HAS NOT ARISEN A PROPHET SINCE IN ISRAEL LIKE MOSES, WHOM THE LORD KNEW FACE TO FACE, NONE LIKE HIM FOR ALL THE SIGNS AND THE WONDERS WHICH THE LORD SENT HIM TO DO IN THE LAND OF EGYPT, TO PHARAOH AND TO ALL HIS SERVANTS AND TO ALL HIS LAND, AND FOR ALL THE MIGHTY POWER AND ALL THE GREAT AND TERRIBLE DEEDS WHICH MOSES WROUGHT IN THE SIGHT OF ALL ISRAEL" (DEUT 34:10-12).

Within Judaism, Moses is widely considered to be the greatest prophet, often called Moshe Rabbeinu, or "Moses, Teacher/Rabbi." And the closing words of the fifth book of the Pentateuch indicate why: because Moses knew God "face to face"; he had an intimate relationship with God, who had revealed to Moses his name from out of the burning bush (Ex. 3). The greatness of Moses was not due to miracles or other deeds, says Benedict; no, the "most important thing is that he spoke with God as with a friend." This shows, Benedict emphasizes, that a true Israelite prophet was not a fortune-teller or a soothsayer:

"His task is not to report on the events of tomorrow or the next day in order to satisfy human curiosity or the human need for security. He shows us the face of God, and in so doing he shows us the path that we have to take. … He points out the path to the true 'exodus,' which consists in this: Among all the paths of history, the path to God is the true direction that we must seek and find. Prophecy in this sense is a strict corollary to Israel's monotheism. It is the translation of this faith into the everyday life of a community before God and on the way to him" (p. 4).

This summarizes many of the points addressed in Lesson 3, including how the prophet warns against—even rails against—finding security in idolatrous substitutes for God. Yet while the prophet may speak of impending doom and he may warn of coming curses, it is always for a single purpose: that the people might return to the path of life, of communion with God, the source of all life and love.

† THE PERFECT PROPHET

As we've seen, Moses and the other Old Testament prophets had a distinctive relationship with God and with the word of God. We've noted how the prophet is identified by three characteristics: he is chosen by God to announce God's word; he is an obedient servant of God's word; and he is shaped by God's word for the sake of God's people. Yet even Moses, the greatest prophet, could not look directly upon the full glory of God. Although Moses is described as speaking "face to face" with God, the book of Exodus also recounts that when Moses requested to see God's glory, he was told: "You cannot see my face; for man shall not see me and live" (see Ex. 33:11, 18-23). Moses was a mediator of the covenant, but there were limits to what he could see and bear.

The future prophet spoken of by Moses would have no such limitations. Quite the contrary, as the prologue of John's Gospel declares: "For the law was given through Moses; grace and truth came through Jesus Christ. No one has ever seen God; the only Son, who is in the bosom of the Father, he has made him known" (Jn. 1:17-18). Jesus, the new and final Prophet, has not only seen God, he is God. The Incarnate Word is obedient unto death, "taking the form of a servant, being born in the likeness of men" (Phil. 2:6-8). And, rather than being shaped by God's word for the sake of God's people, he is the perfect Word of God who takes on flesh for the sake of the world and the people of God.

Put another way, while all of the previous prophets were given God's word, Jesus is a prophet precisely because he is the Word of God: "In the beginning was the Word, and the Word was with God, and the Word was God. He was in the beginning with God..." (Jn. 1:1-2). Or, as Bishop Barron says, "This means Jesus doesn't just speak about the divine truth; he is the divine pattern in person."

All of this is summed up, as we saw at the end of the last chapter, in the opening verses of the Epistle to the Hebrews: "In many and various ways God spoke of old to our fathers by the prophets, but in these last days he has spoken to us by a Son" (Heb. 1:1-2). *The Catechism of the Catholic Church*, remarking on that passage, quotes St. John of the Cross:

> "In giving us his Son, his only Word (for he possesses no other),
> he spoke everything to us at once in this sole Word—and he has
> no more to say ... because what he spoke before to the prophets in
> parts, he has now spoken all at once by giving us the All Who is
> His Son. Any person questioning God or desiring some vision or
> revelation would be guilty not only of foolish behavior but also of
> offending him, by not fixing his eyes entirely upon Christ and by
> living with the desire for some other novelty" (CCC, par. 65).

There is a temptation to constrict Jesus' prophetic work to his words about the future, such as in the Olivet Discourse (Matthew 24, Mark 13, Luke 21). But Jesus' prophetic ministry involved a variety of teachings and actions, some of which were immediately identified and recognized as prophetic in nature. For instance, in the Gospel of Matthew, the crowds said, "This is the prophet Jesus from Nazareth of Galilee" (Matt. 21:11). In the Gospel of Mark, some thought Jesus was the prophet Elijah, sent again by God (as some Jews believed he would be), while others said, "It is a prophet, like one of the prophets of old" (Mk. 6:15). After Jesus brought back to life the son of the widow in Nain, "Fear seized them all; and they glorified God, saying, 'A great prophet has arisen among us!' and 'God has visited his people!'" (Lk. 7:16)

Many of those of who recognized Jesus as a prophet were outcasts, or not even Jewish. After Jesus had remarked about her marriages and relational discord, the Samaritan woman exclaimed, "Sir, I perceive that you are a prophet" (Jn. 4:19). She and others from her town would later confess him to be "the Savior of the world" (Jn. 4:42). The man born blind, having been healed by Jesus and then enduring questioning by the Pharisees, said, "He is a prophet." He would later, upon seeing Jesus again, fall on his knees in adoration, saying, "Lord, I believe" (Jn. 9:17, 38).

While the priestly work of Jesus was not obvious prior to his Passion and death (and would require time to be more deeply appreciated, as the Epistle to the Hebrews indicates) and the exact nature of his kingship was often misunderstood or misrepresented, his prophetic work and words seemed much more direct and accessible. When he was rejected by his countrymen, Jesus explicitly identified himself with the prophets of the Jewish Scriptures, saying, "A prophet is not without honor except in his own country and in his own house" (Matt. 13:57). And, the Evangelist states, Jesus would not perform "mighty works there, because of their unbelief." The mightiest deed, of course, would be his Resurrection, which we will discuss further.

† THE GREAT PROPHETIC DISCOURSE

First, however, we will consider Jesus' great prophetic discourse, the Sermon on the Mount. Describing it as a prophetic discourse might sound strange, especially if prophecy is limited to fore-telling the future. But prophecy, again, is rooted in *forth-telling* the truth about God, the covenant, the law, and the nature of salvation. Again in *Jesus of Nazareth: From the Baptism in the Jordan to the Transfiguration* (Doubleday, 2007), Benedict XVI writes about the Sermon on the Mount, which takes up three chapters in the Gospel of Matthew (5-7). He states, "With this great discourse, Matthew puts together a picture of Jesus as a new Moses in precisely the profound sense that we saw earlier in connection with the promise of a new prophet in the Book of Deuteronomy" (p. 65). The opening verses of Matthew 5 indicate the connection: "Seeing the crowds, he went up on the mountain, and when he sat down his disciples came to him. And he opened his mouth and taught them, saying..." (Mt. 5:1-2). Having already chosen twelve men, who represent the new Israel (Mt. 4:17-22; 10:2), he went up the mountain (a "new Sinai," says Benedict) and took a position of teaching authority. Jesus then delivered the new law, the new Torah:

"It should be clear by now that the Sermon on the Mount is the new Torah brought by Jesus. Moses could deliver his Torah only by entering into the divine darkness on the

mountain. Jesus' Torah likewise presupposes his entering into communion with the Father, the inward ascents of his life, which are then prolonged in his descent into communion of life and suffering with men" (p. 68).

This event took place outside of Jerusalem and the populated areas; it was purposefully detached from the busy-ness and self-centeredness of man, as Erasmo Leiva-Merikakis explains in his commentary *Fire of Mercy, Heart of the World* (Ignatius Press, 1996):

"In presenting this new 'decalogue' to the world, Jesus withdraws from Jerusalem and from all habitations and conventions of men, just as Moses and the Israelites had forsaken Egypt to dwell in the desert, there to receive the divine Law. The scenario is purely elemental and cosmic, comprising only the sky, the earth, and the voice of the incarnate Word. God had given the Decalogue of the Law that condemns to Moses on Mount Sinai amidst thunder and lightning. Here Jesus gives his intimate disciples the ten invitations to perfect love, seated with them on the scrub. The earth itself serves as his throne, as the psalms predicated. Jesus is not only the new Moses but God himself, who inscribes the Law of his Sacred Heart no longer now on stone tablets but on the very hearts of men" (p. 181; cf. Jer. 31:31-33).

The Sermon on the Mount, then, is the prophetic declaration of the new law by God himself—in the flesh, face to face with humanity. And the Beatitudes (Mt. 5:3-12) form the heart of Jesus' great prophetic teaching; as such, they point to heart of his entire mission: his saving work on the cross. "He who climbed the first [mountain] to preach the Beatitudes," wrote Fulton Sheen in his *Life of Christ* (New York, 1958), "must necessarily climb the second to practice what He preached. ... The Sermon on the Mount cannot be separated from His Crucifixion, any more than day can be separated from night" (p. 115).

All of this is rather counterintuitive, and the jarring nature of the new Torah is evidenced precisely in how Jesus spoke of being "blessed," or "happy." Those words, especially "happy," have fairly superficial meanings in our culture today, often associated with good feelings, comfort and pleasure, and lack of suffering and want. But true happiness—real blessedness—is found not in emotions or physical pleasures, but in communion with God. In fact, as Bishop Barron emphasizes, the Beatitudes are meant to free us from those emotions and pleasures that can lead to faulty perspectives and even to damaging addictions. Those addictions, again, are usually found in the four substitutes for God and true happiness: wealth, pleasure, power, and honor.

Is wealth your substitute for God? "Blessed are the poor in spirit," says Jesus (Matt. 5:3). Pope Francis, in his "Message for the Twenty-Ninth World Youth Day," remarked directly on this particular Beatitude:

> "Jesus is God who strips himself of his glory. Here we see God's choice to be poor: he was rich and yet he became poor in order to enrich us through his poverty (cf. 2 Cor 8:9). This is the mystery we contemplate in the crib when we see the Son of God lying in a manger, and later on the cross, where his self-emptying reaches its culmination.
>
> The Greek adjective *ptochós* (poor) does not have a purely material meaning. It means 'a beggar,' and it should be seen as linked to the Jewish notion of the *anawim*, 'God's poor.' It suggests lowliness, a sense of one's limitations and existential poverty. The *anawim* trust in the Lord, and they know that they can count on him."

We are blessed and fortunate, then, to be detached from wealth and material possessions. In the words of St. Ignatius of Loyola: "Lord whether I have a long life or a short life, whether I am healthy or sick, whether I am rich or poor, is a matter of indifference to me, as long as I am following your will."

The antidote for pleasure? "Blessed are those who mourn..." (Matt. 5:4). Whatever does that mean? Consider how fortunate we are to not be attached to emotions and good feelings when it comes to being happy. Good feelings and pleasure can be just as addictive as wealth and power, keeping us from seeing the truly sorrowful and fallen state of man without God. Those who mourn—especially those who mourn for their sins—know that suffering, however intense, cannot destroy the divine life. There's nothing wrong with sensual pleasure, in the proper context and at the proper time. But there is plenty wrong with turning sensual pleasure into your god. When we are too comfortable, we risk becoming indifferent to our sins—and that is a curse.

If power tempts us, or is the altar at the center of our lives, we can ponder these words of Christ: "Blessed are the meek, for they shall inherit the earth" (Matt. 5:5). This goes against the grain of our nature, in part because we perceive meekness to be weakness, a lack of courage or strength. However, the prophet Moses was praised for being meek (Num. 12:3), King David wrote that God will "hear the desire of the meek" (Psa. 10:17), and the prophet Isaiah proclaimed, "The meek shall obtain fresh joy in the LORD…" (Isa. 29:19). Jesus described himself as meek, or gentle and lowly of heart (Matt. 11:29). Meekness is actually true strength; it is humility and gentleness in the face of provocation and danger. The meek renounce power and earthly glory. And the perfect example of this sacrificial meekness is given on the cross by the suffering, selfless Christ.

Finally, there is the temptation—the poison—of honor. "Blessed are those who are persecuted for righteousness' sake," says Jesus, "for theirs is the kingdom of heaven. Blessed are you when men revile you and persecute you and utter all kinds of evil against you falsely on my account" (Matt. 5:10-11). It sounds quite foreign to us. But the Prophet of prophets knows the source of true happiness, and he knows all about persecution, mockery, and hate. Think of it this way: how lucky are those who are not reliant upon the opinions of others and addicted to their approval. This is a sign of hope, for it demonstrates the proper detachment from worldly approval and honors.

Benedict XVI describes the Beatitudes as statements "meant to list practical, but also theological, attributes of the disciples of Jesus—of those who have set out to follow Jesus and have become his family" (*Jesus of Nazareth*, p. 71). They are paradoxical in nature, for the standards of the world, when seen in the light of the Beatitudes, are shown to be upside down, lacking, and contrary to the Christian calling. When we see the world and reality from God's perspective and begin to live in that perspective, we will find joy and meaning amid the trials and struggles of everyday existence. The Beatitudes teach us the real meaning of discipleship and they free us from whatever impedes our love for God, our walk with Christ, and our growth in the Holy Spirit.

Put another way, the Beatitudes are prophetic guides to spiritual life and right worship. Once we are free of our addictions to wealth, pleasure, power, and honor, then we can become properly aligned unto God. St. Paul exhorts the Christians in Rome: "Do not be conformed to this world but be transformed by the renewal of your mind, that you may prove what is the will of God, what is good and acceptable and perfect" (Rom. 12:1-2). That is the goal of the Beatitudes and the Sermon on the Mount. And, looking back at the writings of the Old Testament prophets, that call to embrace sacrifice and to be transformed by the grace of God for glory of God is essential to the work of the true prophet.

Dr. Matthew Levering, in *Christ's Fulfillment of Torah and Temple* (University of Notre Dame, 2002), a study of the theology of St. Thomas Aquinas, writes:

> "Christ is first and foremost the one who reveals the mystery of the Trinity and of human salvation to the world. In this respect, he was a prophet, although, unlike Moses—who Aquinas considers to be the greatest Old Testament prophet—he did not give an exterior law but rather, by the power and truth of his preaching, converted people interiorly through the grace of the Holy Spirit (this interior conversion to the truth is itself a "New Law). … By approaching Christ and receiving his friendship, we come to know his Godhead through his human nature, as befits the fact that our intellects rely on sensibles" (pp. 43, 44).

Again, we see that Christ's prophetic work is intimately connected to the Incarnation; it flows from it and is rooted in it. And the Incarnation leads, firmly and without wavering, to the cross. Bishop Barron reminds us of St. Thomas Aquinas' comments: "If you want to see the full exemplification of the Beatitudes, look to Christ crucified." And also: "Love what he loved on the cross and despise what he despised on the cross, and you'll be happy." Christ crucified, naked and nailed to the cross, has nothing; he is free of wealth, removed from pleasure, powerless, and stripped of any honor. In that state—mocked and reviled by the world—he fulfilled his prophetic work by offering the definitive sign of perfect abandonment, love, and sacrifice.

✝ THE SUFFERING PROPHET

Jesus understood his approaching suffering and death as both a sharing in and a definitive fulfillment of the sufferings underwent by all the prophets before him. Thus, he spoke of his future Passion in prophetic terms. When some of the scribes and Pharisees requested a sign, Jesus used the occasion to prophesy about his approaching confrontation with the grave and death:

> "Then some of the scribes and Pharisees said to him, 'Teacher, we wish to see a sign from you.' But he answered them, "An evil and adulterous generation seeks for a sign; but no sign shall be given to it except the sign of the prophet Jonah. For as Jonah was three days and three nights in the belly of the whale, so will the Son of man be three days and three nights in the heart of the earth" (Matt. 12:38-40).

Like Jonah, Jesus was a prophet sent by God, and he was to bring news of salvation to Gentiles. He would also spend three days entombed. But Jesus was greater than Jonah, not least because he would overcome death, opening the way to salvation and communion with the Father. Reflecting on the work yet to be done, he declared:

> "Nevertheless I must go on my way today and tomorrow and the day following; for it cannot be that a prophet should perish away from Jerusalem.' O Jerusalem, Jerusalem, killing the prophets and stoning those who are sent to you! How often would I have gathered your children together as a hen gathers her brood under her wings, and you would not!" (Lk. 13:33-34; cf. Matt. 23:37-39)

The connection between suffering and the prophetic office is made often in the Gospels, and its importance cannot be overstated. The Old Testament prophets, with few exceptions, suffered deeply because of their work; it was, from a worldly perspective, a thankless task. But, of course, it was a task of eternal consequence.

The prophetic embrace of humble suffering takes on profound meaning in the person of Jesus Christ, for it is the radical culmination of God's loving condescension.

This "divine condescension" (CCC, 684) is an astounding display of God's love. "The motive of this self-abasement is specified," writes Cardinal Christoph Schönborn in *God Sent His Son: A Contemporary Christology* (Ignatius Press, 2010). "God makes himself like the lowliest of men, so that man can give assent to God in complete freedom and not be overwhelmed by the greatness of his majesty. God respects man's freedom to such an extent that he addresses the freedom of man through his self-abasement" (p. 113). As Cardinal Schönborn explains further, not only does God humble himself, he does so that we can be raised up into a new life of grace. The prophets provided a foreshadowing of this glorious truth because, rather than being passive vessels of divine utterance, they were called into a remarkable and personal relationship with God. They were human representatives who proclaimed not only the judgment, but also the mercy and love of God.

Yet the prophets, because they were so close to God, often had to suffer, and in doing so gave expression to God's own sorrow. In becoming man and dwelling among us, God took this prophetic work to a new and startling level. Jesus Christ is not just another human representative who is close to God, but is God-made-flesh, the Son who perfectly and fully represents the Father. God, having become man, suffers as a man; he endures rejection, vilification, mockery, torture, and then death.

Jesus' prophetic insight into this fact is evident in the parable of the vineyard (Mk. 12:1-9), in which he describes a landowner who sends servants to the tenants, seeking to collect the landowner's portion of the harvest. The servants are beaten and wounded, and even killed. Then the landowner sends his "beloved son," saying, "They will respect my son." But they kill him, too, and "cast him out of the vineyard." The servants represent the many prophets of old; the beloved son is Jesus himself.

When Peter gave his sermon in Solomon's portico (Act 3:11-26), alongside the Temple, he emphasized the suffering and death of Jesus, the Resurrection, and Jesus' identity as the prophet foretold by Moses. God, declared the head apostle, has "glorified his servant Jesus," yet the people had denied Jesus, and so the "Author of life" was killed. Yet he was vindicated, for God raised him from the dead. However, his suffering had been foretold, for the Christ was a suffering prophet, and he was the final prophet spoken of by the greatest prophet of the Jewish Scriptures:

"Moses said, 'The Lord God will raise up for you a prophet from your brethren as he raised me up. You shall listen to him in whatever he tells you. And it shall be that every soul that does not listen to that prophet shall be destroyed from the people.' And all the prophets who have spoken, from Samuel and those who came afterwards, also proclaimed these days. You are the sons of the prophets and of the covenant which God gave to your fathers, saying to Abraham, 'And in your posterity shall all the families of the earth be blessed'" (Act 3:22-25).

This same declaration was also made, in the Acts of the Apostles, by the first martyr, Stephen: "Which of the prophets did not your fathers persecute? And they killed those who announced beforehand the coming of the Righteous One, whom you have now betrayed and murdered..." (Acts 7:52; see v. 37). Persecution and suffering, wrote Jean Daniélou in *The Advent of Salvation* (Deus Books, 1962), seem "to be absolutely of the essence of the prophet, for being the witness and instrument of God's ways. Men want to arrange history to fit in with their limited earthly vision, which is quite different from God's view of things. The prophet, therefore, who represents God's outlook, cuts across the plans that men are making; and that is why they reject him" (p. 184).

† SHARING IN CHRIST'S PROPHETIC OFFICE

The fathers of the Second Vatican Council reflected on how all Catholics, including laity, participate in Christ's prophetic office:

"The holy people of God shares also in Christ's prophetic office; it spreads abroad a living witness to Him, especially by means of a life of faith and charity and by offering to God a sacrifice of praise, the tribute of lips which give praise to His name. ... Christ, the great Prophet, who proclaimed the Kingdom of His Father both by the testimony of His life and the power of His words, continually fulfills

His prophetic office until the complete manifestation of glory. He does this not only through the hierarchy who teach in His name and with His authority, but also through the laity whom He made His witnesses and to whom He gave understanding of the faith (sensu fidei) and an attractiveness in speech so that the power of the Gospel might shine forth in their daily social and family life. They conduct themselves as children of the promise, and thus strong in faith and in hope they make the most of the present, and with patience await the glory that is to come. Let them not, then, hide this hope in the depths of their hearts, but even in the program of their secular life let them express it by a continual conversion and by wrestling 'against the world-rulers of this darkness, against the spiritual forces of wickedness'" (*Lumen Gentium*, pars. 12, 35).

The conciliar fathers specifically mention the prophetic function of marriage and family life: "For where Christianity pervades the entire mode of family life, and gradually transforms it, one will find there both the practice and an excellent school of the lay apostolate." The family proclaims the virtues of the Kingdom, as well as the "hope of a blessed life to come." And then there is this rather striking statement: "Thus by its example and its witness it accuses the world of sin and enlightens those who seek the truth." That, of course, is what Jesus did in his public ministry. It should be no surprise that those who have been baptized into the death and Resurrection of the suffering, crucified, and risen Christ would be asked to do the same.

The laity, in short, are to share the Gospel in the world in ways that the hierarchy and clergy are not able to. This work of lay evangelization, which is rooted in the sacraments of baptism and confirmation, bears a distinct character, as Pope Paul VI explained in *Evangelii Nuntiandi*:

> "Lay people, whose particular vocation places them in the midst of the world and in charge of the most varied temporal tasks, must for this very reason exercise a very special form of evangelization.

> Their primary and immediate task is not to establish and develop the ecclesial community—this is the specific role of the pastors—but to put to use every Christian and evangelical possibility latent but already present and active in the affairs of the world. Their own field of evangelizing activity is the vast and complicated world of politics, society and economics, but also the world of culture, of the sciences and the arts, of international life, of the mass media. It also includes other realities which are open to evangelization, such as human love, the family, the education of children and adoles-

cents, professional work, suffering. The more Gospel-inspired lay people there are engaged in these realities, clearly involved in them, competent to promote them and conscious that they must exercise to the full their Christian powers which are often buried and suffocated, the more these realities will be at the service of the kingdom of God and therefore of salvation in Jesus Christ, without in any way losing or sacrificing their human content but rather pointing to a transcendent dimension which is often disregarded" (par. 70).

The challenges involved are daunting. But they always have been. The lives and witness of the prophets demonstrate how hard it can be to embrace and proclaim the word of God in the world. Yet we also know that the Word became flesh and dwelt among us so that we can enter into his divine life and live it fully in this world, without fear or compromise, for the glory of God.

Lesson Four: QUESTIONS FOR UNDERSTANDING

Please use the commentary above and the references listed with each question to develop your answers.

1. Why is Moses considered the greatest prophet of the Old Testament? (Exodus 3:11-17;

   Deut 18:15-16 and 34:10-12)

2. How is Jesus the great and final prophet promised through Moses? (John 1:1-2 and 1:17-18;

   Philippians 2:6-11; Hebrews 1:1-2; CCC 65, 2858)

3. What are some examples from the Gospels of people proclaiming Jesus as a prophet?

4. In what ways does Matthew indicate that the Sermon on the Mount is a prophetic discourse revealing Jesus to be the new Moses? (Matthew 5:1-2; Jeremiah 31:31-34; CCC 581, 2056)

5. How do the laity participate in the prophetic office of Christ? (CCC 1241)

Lesson Four: QUESTIONS FOR APPLICATION

1. If Moses was the greatest prophet of the Old Testament because of his close relationship with God, what does that indicate about those who have been baptized into Christ and filled with the Holy Spirit?

2. In what ways has God called you to be prophetic in your everyday life?

3. How are you sometimes distracted from your prophetic calling?

   What temptations most impede your growth as a witness to the Gospel?

4. How does the example of Christ help you to overcome impediments and temptations?

5. In what way might sufferings in your life be an opportunity to more deeply and richly embrace the prophetic mission entrusted to us by Jesus?

NOTES

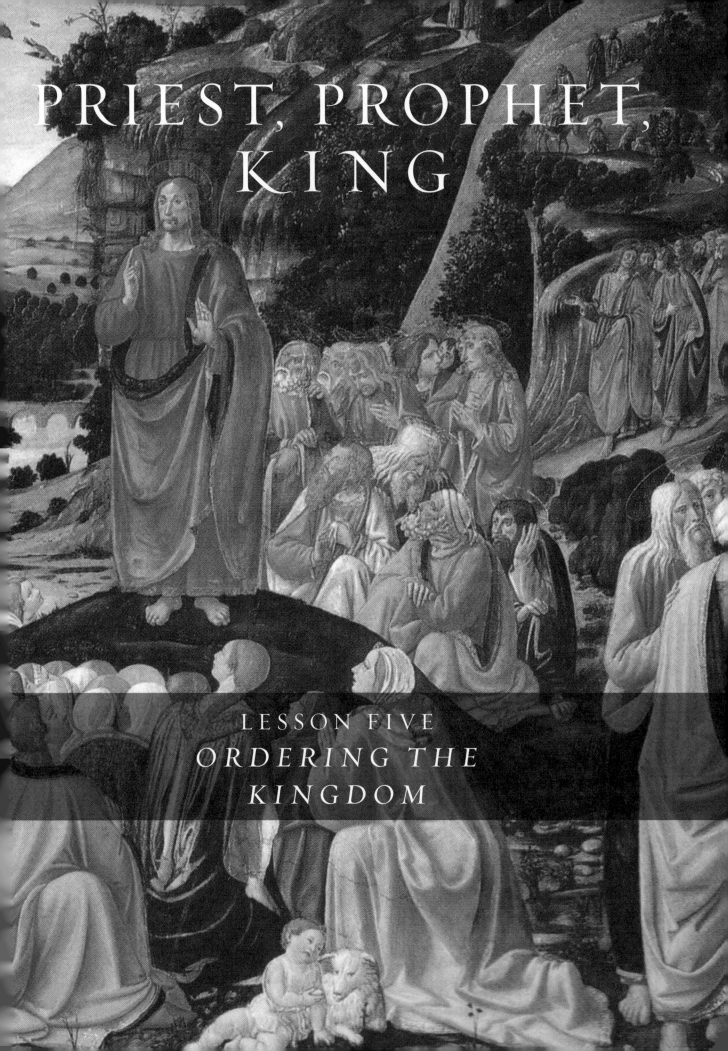

PRIEST, PROPHET, KING

LESSON FIVE
ORDERING THE KINGDOM

ORDERING THE KINGDOM
LESSON FIVE VIDEO OUTLINE

I.   ROLE OF THE KING

    A. Orders the people of God

    B. Orders the charisms of the people

II. KING DAVID'S STRENGTH

    A. Chosen by God and annointed as king in the Old Testament

       1. "Christos" in Greek

       2. "Mashiach" in Hebrew

    B. Listens to God

    C. "Sweet singer of Israel": Articulator of Israel's vision in beautiful speech

    D. Unites the nation of Israel

       1. Makes Jerusalem the capital

       2. Installs the Ark of the Covenant in the Temple

       3. Leads the people in the right praise of God

    E. Warrior/fighter

       1. Akin to all Old Testament kings

       2. All the battles and militaristic maneuvers point to the true king opposing all powers that are opposed to God as a foreshadowing of Jesus, the King of kings.

       3. Follows God's directive to "put the ban on those powers" and fight them all the way to extinction, as we are to fight evil thoroughly

III. KING DAVID'S WEAKNESS

    A. Gets a little lazy and does not campaign vigorously against the enemies of Israel and of God

    B. Uses his kingly power to claim Bathsheba for his wife; has her husband killed

    C. All of Israel suffers due to his lapse in kingship

IV. ALL BAPTIZED CALLED TO BE KINGS

    A. Rule ourselves, families, and communities according to God's will

    B. When we rule according to our ego, all suffer

LESSON FIVE

ORDERING THE KINGDOM

For Americans and others living under democracy, the concept of a king can seem quite foreign, quaint, and curious—perhaps even silly. The United States was formed directly in opposition to rule by a king, and the past century witnessed the end of many kingdoms. Those that do exist, at least in the West, are mostly ceremonial in nature. "In a few years," said King Farouk I of Egypt in 1950, "there will only be five kings in the world—the king of England and the four kings in a pack of cards." He wasn't far off!

Sacred Scripture, in contrast, is filled with numerous references to kings. In fact, it's safe to say that kings are the most mentioned group of men in the entire Bible. "The king was the central and key figure in the life and affairs of the Israelite nation," observes Dr. Aaron Chalmers in *Exploring the Religion of Ancient Israel: Prophet, Priest, Sage & People* (InterVarsity Press, 2012). "He exercised some degree of power over virtually every aspect of the nation's existence, whether economic, political or social. Generally speaking, however, Western readers of the Bible have tended to neglect or downplay the role of the king in Israel's religious life" (p. 89).

Why is that so? Chalmers offers two reasons. First, the modern West tends to emphasize the separation of Church and State, which has contributed to the separation of the sacred and secular realms. This has caused many readers to view the ancient Israelite kings in solely political terms. But those kings were religious leaders as well as political leaders, as we will see in the life of the most famous Old Testament king, David.

Secondly, the Old Testament itself, in various ways, downplays "the religious responsibilities of Israel's kings. For example, the cultic regulations found in Leviticus give no special place to the king, suggesting that he was viewed as a standard member of the laity without any special or unique prerogatives." The two books that *do* depict David, Solomon, and other kings playing key roles in the liturgy and worship of Israel—1 and II Chronicles—are among the least read books in the Bible! However, a glance at some numbers suggests how important the role and office of the king is in

Scripture. While the descriptive "prophet" occurs less than 300 times in the Old and New Testaments and the title of "priest" around 500 times, the Bible features about 2,700 uses of the Hebrew word *melek* and around 125 uses of the Greek word *basileus*, both of which are translated as "king."

† GOD THE KING

An understanding and proclamation of the eternal kingship of God appears quite often in the Old Testament. While the term "kingdom of God" is not explicitly used in the Old Testament, the idea is clearly expressed in various ways. In Exodus 15, Moses declares the strength and might of God:

> "THY RIGHT HAND, O LORD, GLORIOUS IN POWER, THY RIGHT HAND, O LORD, SHATTERS THE ENEMY. IN THE GREATNESS OF THY MAJESTY THOU OVERTHROWEST THY ADVERSARIES; THOU SENDEST FORTH THY FURY, IT CONSUMES THEM LIKE STUBBLE" (Ex. 15:6-7).

Later Moses states: "The LORD will reign for ever and ever" (Ex. 15:18). God's kingdom, says King David in one of his many Psalms, shines forth in glory and power: "Thy kingdom is an everlasting kingdom, and thy dominion endures throughout all generations. The LORD is faithful in all his words, and gracious in all his deeds" (Psa. 145:10-13). This theme of God's everlasting kingdom, or reign, is prominent in several other Psalms:

- "The LORD is king for ever and ever; the nations shall perish from his land" (Psa. 10:16).

- "The LORD sits enthroned over the flood; the LORD sits enthroned as king for ever" (Psa. 29:10).

- "For the LORD is a great God, and a great King above all gods" (Psa. 95:3).

- "The LORD has established his throne in the heavens, and his kingdom rules over all" (Psa. 103:19).

- "The LORD will reign for ever, thy God, O Zion, to all generations. Praise the LORD!" (Psa. 146:10)

The prophet Jeremiah describes God as "the living God and the everlasting King" (Jer. 10:10) and the prophet Isaiah, given a vision of the throne room of God, exclaims, "Woe is me! For I am lost; for I am a man of unclean lips, and I dwell in the midst of a people of unclean lips; for my eyes have seen the King, the LORD of hosts!" (Isa. 6:5) Zechariah, prophesying of the coming "day of the Lord," states, "And the LORD will become king over all the earth; on that day the LORD will be one and his name one" (Zech. 14:9).

God is praised as king in many Old Testament passages for liberating and guiding the chosen people at key moments. The Exodus from Egypt and the crossing of the Red Sea, one of the most significant and defining moments in the history of the Jews, is one such event. The entire Song of Moses in Exodus 15 is a declaration of God's strength, power, majesty, and glory. God is described as the one who "shatters the enemy," who is "majestic in holiness" and "terrible in glorious deeds," and yet also acts out of "steadfast love" for the people he has redeemed, bought back out of slavery.

Essential to understanding the kingship of God is the Oneness and Otherness of God, as well as his unique, covenantal relationship with the nation of Israel, formed at Mount Sinai following the liberation from Egypt. Both are evident in the giving of the Decalogue, or Ten Commandments. Freedom from Egyptian slavery was, as the *Catechism* explains, "the great liberating event at the center of the Old Covenant." All of the commandments set forth "the conditions of a life freed from the slavery of sin" (CCC 2057).

God's kingly deliverance initiated the Mosaic covenant, which forged a new relationship, and the Ten Commandments and the Law, which regulated and perpetuated that relationship. Exodus 19 offers a succinct description of the covenant, uttered by God to Moses:

> "THEREFORE, IF YOU HEARKEN TO MY VOICE AND KEEP MY COVENANT, YOU SHALL BE MY SPECIAL POSSESSION, DEARER TO ME THAN ALL OTHER PEOPLE, THOUGH ALL THE EARTH IS MINE. YOU SHALL BE TO ME A KINGDOM OF PRIESTS, A HOLY NATION. THAT IS WHAT YOU MUST TELL THE ISRAELITES" (Ex 19:5-6).

This relationship was not merely legal or judicial, but personal and moral. This is noteworthy because the Jews believed that God's reign took place on three levels, or within three types of relationship: with each person on an individual level, with the chosen people as a group, and then with the entire world. Moses, the great prophet, gave witness to all three forms of God's rule, for he was directly chosen and commanded by God (Ex. 3), he mediated God's covenant with the people (Ex. 19), and he told Pharaoh on behalf of God that the Egyptian ruler would be spared: "For this

purpose have I let you live, to show you my power, so that my name may be declared throughout all the earth" (Ex. 19:16).

The commandments given to Moses provided the Israelites with a moral framework for understanding and maintaining the covenantal relationship—a binding agreement that was the heart of the life-giving and protecting bond between a king and his people in the Ancient Near Eastern world. Ten Commandments were meant to lead to the fullness of life and to possession of the Promised Land. Rather than blind submission to an unknown divine power, the people were to respond with love to the mercy and goodness of the Lord, whose rule and reign was not tyrannical, but moral and even marital. "The Commandments properly so-called," states the *Catechism*, "come in the second place: they express the implications of belonging to God through the establishment of the covenant. Moral existence is a response to the Lord's loving initiative" (CCC 2062).

Although it is commonplace to hear the Ten Commandments spoken of as being rigid or even based in anger, they are deeply personal and flow from a momentous expression of divine, personal love. God's creation of the cosmos, the world, and everything in the world was due to His love. "Creation is revealed as the first step towards this covenant, the first and universal witness to God's all-powerful love" (CCC 288).

† KINGSHIP IN ISRAEL

Throughout the historical books, God is shown to be king over all the false gods (especially Baal, who is a constant temptation to the Israelites), king over Israel, and king over all the nations. While the numerous gods of the surrounding nations were local deities, bound to a specific place, tree, or mountain, the true God was not limited in such a way, nor could he be known (and thus controlled, at least to some extent) as could the pagan gods and goddesses. God was, as he showed Moses, uniquely intimate and personal, as well as completely mysterious and "other." The *Catechism* reflects on this vital point with these words of explanation and caution:

"God transcends all creatures. We must therefore continually purify our language of everything in it that is limited, image-bound or imperfect, if we are not to confuse our image of God—'the inexpressible, the incomprehensible, the invisible, the ungraspable'—with our human representations. Our human words always fall short of the mystery of God" (CCC 42).

The people of Israel had to constantly battle the temptation to either understand God in a skewed fashion or to simply worship false gods. And once they had settled in the land and began to establish themselves in a permanent fashion, there was also a growing desire to have a king, as did the surrounding nations. The relationship between God the King and the various kings of Israel was often difficult and even contentious. The main reason was that a king faced powerful temptations and serious dangers inherent to centralized and concentrated power. The book of Deuteronomy, which presents an ideal for the kings of Israel, states:

> "WHEN YOU COME TO THE LAND WHICH THE LORD YOUR GOD GIVES YOU, AND YOU POSSESS IT AND DWELL IN IT, AND THEN SAY, 'I WILL SET A KING OVER ME, LIKE ALL THE NATIONS THAT ARE ROUND ABOUT ME'; YOU MAY INDEED SET AS KING OVER YOU HIM WHOM THE LORD YOUR GOD WILL CHOOSE. ONE FROM AMONG YOUR BRETHREN YOU SHALL SET AS KING OVER YOU; YOU MAY NOT PUT A FOREIGNER OVER YOU, WHO IS NOT YOUR BROTHER" (DT. 17:14-15).

The passage then warns of the temptations of power and material possessions that will face every king:

> "ONLY HE MUST NOT MULTIPLY HORSES FOR HIMSELF, OR CAUSE THE PEOPLE TO RETURN TO EGYPT IN ORDER TO MULTIPLY HORSES, SINCE THE LORD HAS SAID TO YOU, 'YOU SHALL NEVER RETURN THAT WAY AGAIN.' AND HE SHALL NOT MULTIPLY WIVES FOR HIMSELF, LEST HIS HEART TURN AWAY; NOR SHALL HE GREATLY MULTIPLY FOR HIMSELF SILVER AND GOLD."

Horses were a tremendous military advantage against foot soldiers, and were thus a temptation to trust in military might rather than in God (cf. Psa. 20:7; Isa. 31:1; Mic. 5:10-15). Having many wives meant marrying into the families of foreign royalty for the sake of political alliances, which in turn meant bringing the idols and gods of those wives into Israel—a serious problem that eventually hastened the ruin of Solomon (1 Kings 11:1-10).

The ideal king, however, wouldn't focus on alliances and political pacts, but on the law and the covenant:

> "And when he sits on the throne of his kingdom, he shall write for himself in a book a copy of this law, from that which is in the charge of the Levitical priests; and it shall be with him, and he shall read in it all the days of his life, that he may learn to fear the Lord his God, by keeping all the words of this law and these statutes, and doing them; that his heart may not be lifted up above his brethren, and that he may not turn aside from the commandment, either to the right hand or to the left; so that he may continue long in his kingdom, he and his children, in Israel" (Deut. 17:18-20).

These admonitions lead to three basic conclusions. First, there was to be a limit to the power of the king, to keep the people from tyranny and the king from assuming a role that only God can fill. Secondly, the king's central responsibility was to protect and facilitate the people's full allegiance to God and the Torah. The law of the king, notes Patrick D. Miller in his commentary on Deuteronomy (*Interpretation series*, John Knox Press, 1990), "is, like all Deuteronomic instruction, a guard against apostasy and idolatry." Third, the king was to be what Miller calls a "model Israelite." The "fundamental task of the leader of the people, therefore, is to exemplify and demonstrate true obedience to the Lord for the sake of the well-being of both the dynasty and the kingdom. King and subject share a common goal: to learn to fear the Lord" (pp. 148-149).

† KING DAVID

Which brings us to David, the greatest king of Israel, whose many accomplishments (and failings) are described in 1 and 2 Samuel, as well as in 1 and 2 Chronicles. The books of Samuel are especially important, for they describe Israel's transition from a confederation of twelve tribes to a kingdom, spanning about seventy years or so (c. 1040 BC – 970 BC). As Fr. Michael Duggan notes in *The Consuming Fire* (Ignatius Press, 1991), his study of the Old Testament, the "Israelites' pathway toward nationhood advanced in three successive stages corresponding to the careers of its three great leaders" (p. 170): the prophet Samuel, King Saul, and King David.

Under Samuel (1040-1020 BC), the loose confederation of tribes was shaped into a single body; the prophet was both a spiritual and political leader—a judge—and he was the one who eventually anointed the first kings of Israel (1 Sam. 9:26-10:8; 16:1-13). When Samuel reached old age, after many years of ruling, his sons proved to be inept and corrupt leaders (1 Sam. 8:1-3), which led the elders of Israel to approach Samuel with a surprising, but not completely unexpected, demand:

> "'Behold, you are old and your sons do not walk in your ways; now appoint for us a king to govern us like all the nations.' But the thing displeased Samuel when they said, 'Give us a king to govern us.' And Samuel prayed to the LORD. And the LORD said to Samuel, 'Hearken to the voice of the people in all that they say to you; for they have not rejected you, but they have rejected me from being king over them. According to all the deeds which they have done to me, from the day I brought them up out of Egypt even to this day, forsaking me and serving other gods, so they are also doing to you. Now then, hearken to their voice; only, you shall solemnly warn them, and show them the ways of the king who shall reign over them'" (1 Sam. 8:5-9).

This indicates an ambivalence about earthly kings that is a regular theme in the Old Testament. On the one hand, having a king made sense, especially when it came to governance and military leadership; on the other hand, the many temptations that came with kingship would be a constant source of difficulty and even downfall. Samuel warned of the baggage that came with having a king: arrogance, materialism, lust for power, and oppression (1 Sam. 8:10-18). But the people "refused to listen to the voice of Samuel; and they said, 'No! But we will have a king over us, that we also may be like all the nations, and that our king may govern us and go out before us and fight our battles'" (1 Sam. 8:19-20).

Saul, the first king, marked the second stage in the move toward nationhood, for he was a charismatic and gifted military leader, "a handsome young man" from the tribe of Benjamin (1 Sam. 9:1-2). He led a successful and important campaign against the Ammonites (1 Sam. 11), and then carried out campaigns against the Philistines and other enemy tribes (1 Sam. 14). He was acclaimed by Samuel and the people at the start, but tensions soon developed between Saul and Samuel when the young king offered sacrifices that were meant to be offered by the prophet (1 Sam. 13:7-14).

Samuel's condemnation is noteworthy because it speaks to the proper role of the king and indicates what will distinguish Saul's successor:

> "AND SAMUEL SAID TO SAUL, 'YOU HAVE DONE FOOLISHLY; YOU HAVE NOT KEPT THE COMMANDMENT OF THE LORD YOUR GOD, WHICH HE COMMANDED YOU; FOR NOW THE LORD WOULD HAVE ESTABLISHED YOUR KINGDOM OVER ISRAEL FOR EVER. BUT NOW YOUR KINGDOM SHALL NOT CONTINUE; THE LORD HAS SOUGHT OUT A MAN AFTER HIS OWN HEART; AND THE LORD HAS APPOINTED HIM TO BE PRINCE OVER HIS PEOPLE, BECAUSE YOU HAVE NOT KEPT WHAT THE LORD COMMANDED YOU'" (1 SAM. 13:13-14).

The "man after God's own heart" was, of course, David (Acts 13:21-23). As Saul began spiraling into disobedience and jealous rages, David's renown and popularity grew. Saul's biggest failure, as Fr. Duggan observes, is not that he failed, but that he did not address the root problems. "However, Saul's deepest personal failure did not consist in his act of sinning but rather in his refusal to uproot sin from his life. He admitted his sin but did not repent (1 Sam. 15:30)" (p. 175). Saul's religious practices were not based in authentic love for God, but in love of self; when given the chance to truly repent, he refused (1 Sam. 15:16-31). In this regard, Saul and David were completely different, for even when David committed grave sins—including murder and adultery—he admitted his sins, confessed them, and accepted the serious consequences.

Everyone is familiar with the story of the young and bold David killing the Philistine giant, Goliath (1 Sam. 17); nearly everyone is familiar with Psalm 23, perhaps David's most famous psalm. But an essential text for understanding David's relationship with God, as well as appreciating more deeply how Jesus perfectly fulfills the Davidic kingship, is found in 2 Samuel 7. This passage, notes the *New Jerome Biblical Commentary* (Prentice Hall, 1990), "is fundamental in Israelite, Jewish, and Christian royal messianism" (p. 156), for it presents the covenant made with David and points toward God's plans for the kingship of Israel. As such, it became the source of hope for a Messiah, in the mold of David, as expounded by the later prophets and psalmists. The passage states:

"Now therefore thus you shall say to my servant David, 'Thus says the Lord of hosts, I took you from the pasture, from following the sheep, that you should be prince over my people Israel; and I have been with you wherever you went, and have cut off all your enemies from before you; and I will make for you a great name, like the name of the great ones of the earth.

And I will appoint a place for my people Israel, and will plant them, that they may dwell in their own place, and be disturbed no more; and violent men shall afflict them no more, as formerly, from the time that I appointed judges over my people Israel; and I will give you rest from all your enemies. Moreover the Lord declares to you that the Lord will make you a house.

When your days are fulfilled and you lie down with your fathers, I will raise up your offspring after you, who shall come forth from your body, and I will establish his kingdom. He shall build a house for my name, and I will establish the throne of his kingdom for ever. I will be his father, and he shall be my son. When he commits iniquity, I will chasten him with the rod of men, with the stripes of the sons of men; but I will not take my steadfast love from him, as I took it from Saul, whom I put away from before you. And your house and your kingdom shall be made sure for ever before me; your throne shall be established for ever'" (2 Sam. 7:8-16).

This covenant was given through the prophet Nathan. In fact, the prophets were to exercise the authority of God's word over the king, as Fr. Duggan points out: "The prophet discerns the heart of the king and must confront him when he sins. … The prophet works also to protect the people against the excesses and abuses of the king (1 Sam. 8:1-22; 12:1-24)" (p. 178). The covenant with David shows that the former shepherd boy was not just a great military leader and charismatic politician (although he was certainly both), but was a man of God carrying out a divine plan—a plan stretching far into the future. David's great desire, to his everlasting (literally) credit was to build a house, a temple, for God; David's love for God and his desire to worship him properly were remarkable, even if David failed in other ways.

Because of this, and because of God's providential mercy, David was "adopted" by God. And that adoption was an essential part of the Davidic dynasty, for Solomon was also spoken of in the same terms: "He shall build a house for my name. He shall be my son, and I will be his father, and I will

establish his royal throne in Israel for ever" (1 Chron. 22:10). This did not mean that the kings were deified; rather, it meant they were chosen by the one, true, and eternal King, God himself, to eventually bring about the kingdom of God—which is, of course, exactly what Jesus, the Incarnate Son of God, did a millennium after David ruled.

Nathan's presentation of God's covenant with David brought to a climax the various covenants established in the Old Testament: with Noah (Gen. 9:1-17), Abraham (Gen. 17:1-27), and with Moses and all of Israel (Ex. 19:1-24:11). The covenant with David, however, more closely resembles the covenant with Abraham rather than with Moses and Israel at Sinai, for it is unconditional. "The Davidic covenant is one of promise," states Fr. Duggan, "that guarantees fulfillment solely because God is faithful" (p. 179). The unconditional nature of the covenant is vital, for the kings—including David and Solomon, who mark the "golden age" of the Israelite kingdom—repeatedly sinned and failed, often in disturbing and dramatic fashion. When the people were finally taken to Babylon (597-538 BC), the likelihood of a renewed and restored Davidic kingdom must have seemed nearly impossible to the exiled Jews.

† THE DAVIDIC KING & THE KINGDOM OF GOD

This explains why the Chronicler, many years after the Babylonian Exile (c. 400-250 BC), wrote his history of King David and his successors: to assure his readers that God's plan was still in place. As Dr. Scott Hahn explains in *The Kingdom of God as Liturgical Empire* (Baker Academic, 2012), his commentary on 1 and 2 Chronicles, the heart of the Davidic covenant is the promise of divine sonship, to be established through a perfect and righteous king. "The Davidic king is also a new-Adam figure, a son of God who stands as God's vice-regent or prince over creation," writes Hahn. "In David and the kingdom of David, we see a partial or provisional restoration of God's plans for creation... There is a profound identification of the Davidic kingdom with the divine kingship of God" (p. 75). The end-goal is that David's kingship was never an end in itself, but always subordinated "to its true end, the kingship of

God." David's throne is really God's throne, and David's reign is really God's reign, as David himself recognized and proclaimed:

> "Blessed art thou, O Lord, the God of Israel our father, for ever and ever. Thine, O Lord, is the greatness, and the power, and the glory, and the victory, and the majesty; for all that is in the heavens and in the earth is thine; thine is the kingdom, O Lord, and thou art exalted as head above all. Both riches and honor come from thee, and thou rulest over all. In thy hand are power and might; and in thy hand it is to make great and to give strength to all. And now we thank thee, our God, and praise thy glorious name" (1 Chron. 29:10-13).

And so when the Messiah, the Son of David (Mt. 1:1), finally comes, it makes sense—supernatural sense—that he is both truly man (a descendant of David) and truly God, and therefore truly King and Lord of All. Those who enter into the kingdom of God—the "liturgical empire," as Hahn describes it—through baptism, are sharers in the kingship of Christ. As *Lumen Gentium* explains:

> "Christ, becoming obedient even unto death and because of this exalted by the Father, entered into the glory of His kingdom. . . But the Lord wishes to spread His kingdom also by means of the laity, namely, a kingdom of truth and life, a kingdom of holiness and grace, a kingdom of justice, love and peace" (par. 36).

Lesson Five: QUESTIONS FOR UNDERSTANDING

Please use the commentary above and the references listed with each question to develop your answers.

1. How common are references to kings in the Bible, especially in relation to other offices or titles? Why are such references to kings often overlooked or ignored?

2. What are some of the essential qualities and characteristics of God as king in the Old Testament? (Exodus 15; Psa. 145:10-13; 10:16; 29:10; 95:3; 103:19; 146:10)

3. What is a basic definition of a "covenant" or "covenantal relationship" involving a king? How is it connected with the Decalogue, or Ten Commandments? (CCC 2060-63, 2077)

4. What were some of the temptations that came with being a king? In light of those, what were three key characteristics of a good king and kingship? (1 Sam. 8:10-18; Deut. 17:18-20)

5. How did God view the people's desire for an earthly king? What was the main reason for King Saul's eventual failure as king? (1 Sam. 8:5-9 and 13:5-14)

1. When you think of a "king," what comes to mind? What qualities are most important or compelling when you consider God as king? How might contemplating God as king provide hope, solace, or comfort?

2. How is God's covenantal relationship with the people of Israel like a marriage? What does this tell you about the nature of God and his kingship?

3. The kings of Israel were tempted in many ways to ignore or break God's commands. What are some of the lessons that can be learned from their mistakes? What temptations facing us in today's world are similar to the temptations faced in ancient Israel?

4. How was David a "man after God's heart"? What are the qualities of David that most impress, or even inspire you? After reading Psalms 23 and 51, what might you be able to learn from David to help you grow in your relationship with God?

NOTES

PRIEST, PROPHET, KING

KING OF KINGS
LESSON SIX VIDEO OUTLINE

I. JESUS FULFILLS ISRAEL'S LONGING FOR THE DEFINITIVE KING, THE PERFECT DAVID

   A. Descended from David – Gospel of Matthew's genealogy grouped in three sets of 14. In Hebrew, every letter is a number and "David" adds up to 14

   B. Jesus is the perfect king: Listens to the Father; Sweet singer of the truth; unites Israel's 12 tribes (12 apostles), inaugurating the Kingdom of God

   C. Jesus is a warrior-king in a strange, new way

II. JESUS' KINGSHIP

   A. Must break up the bad, dysfunctional forms of community (the Satanic, worldly kingdom) to establish the new Kingdom of God

   B. Sneaks into the world "behind enemy lines" as a poor, humble infant. But the evil powers know that he is the definitive king and they come out in force against him

   C. Jesus leads us out of our sinfulness. Example: human scapegoating patterns

      1. Rene Girard's treatise on age-old way of organizing communities according to one common enemy ("scape-goating mechanism")

      2. Jesus leads with and teaches non-violence, forgiveness and peace

      3. The story of the woman caught in adultery (John 8) illustrates this new way of the King of kings

III. JESUS BECOMES THE ULTIMATE SCAPEGOAT

   A. All forms of accusation and evil come against him

      1. Judas' kiss of betrayal

      2. Peter's denial

      3. Sanhedrin united to accuse Jesus

      4. Pilate and Herod, who were enemies, become friends united against Jesus

B. Pilate is first evangelist proclaiming Jesus as King of the Jews

    1. Jesus stands against scapegoating and for nonviolence, forgiveness, and peace

    2. A new king has come with a new way; Satan's way in conquered

IV. ROLE OF THE BAPTIZED

A. Priest: to reconcile people to God

B. Prophet: to proclaim God's truth. Our faith is not a private matter, so we need to go out and evangelize

C. King: to govern ourselves, our family, and our community according to God's will

D. Follow Jesus and align ourselves with him

E. Let him be king of all parts of ourselves and of our lives

LESSON 6

KING OF KINGS

As we saw in the previous chapter, kings and kingship are mentioned numerous times in the Old Testament, far more than priests, priesthood, and prophets. And yet the office of king was a point of tension and contention for the Jewish people in the period of the judges (c. 1500-1000 B.C.). God was king of the chosen people, and the idea of an earthly king was viewed with deep suspicion. But, eventually, because of the growing strength of Israel's twelve tribes and the poor leadership of Samuel's sons (1 Sam. 8:1-3), the people demanded that the prophet appoint a king (1 Sam 8:6-9).

Saul, the first king, was both charismatic and conflicted. His downfall was due, eventually, to his re-fusal to obey the commands of God and the directives of Samuel; he failed to be the model Israelite and thus failed to be a good and worthy king. David, a "man after God's own heart" (1 Sam. 13:13-14; Acts 13:21-23), had faults and failings, but he was also a man of deep, even mystical, faith in God— committed to worshipping God and building a temple, a house, for the Lord. When David did sin, his remorse and contrition were authentic; he never gave excuses and he didn't try to blame others, unlike Saul (cf. 1 Sam. 15). One of the most revealing and powerful statements by David in this regard is found in Psalm 51, which he wrote after having been confronted by the prophet Nathan over the king's adultery with Bathsheba (2 Sam. 12). After confessing his sins and profess-ing his contrition, David wrote:

> "FOR THOU HAST NO DELIGHT IN SACRIFICE; WERE I TO GIVE A BURNT OFFERING, THOU WOULDST NOT BE PLEASED. THE SACRIFICE ACCEPTABLE TO GOD IS A BROKEN SPIRIT; A BRO-KEN AND CONTRITE HEART, O GOD, THOU WILT NOT DESPISE. DO GOOD TO ZION IN THY GOOD PLEASURE; REBUILD THE WALLS OF JERUSALEM, THEN WILT THOU DELIGHT IN RIGHT SACRIFICES, IN BURNT OFFERINGS AND WHOLE BURNT OFFERINGS; THEN BULLS WILL BE OFFERED ON THY ALTAR" (PSA 51:16-19).

David understood that a true king was first and foremost a servant of God, who alone is the true and perfect king. He also recognized that a king must sacrifice his desires and aspirations for the good of the people and the kingdom; a good king must die to himself and be humble in his ways.

A good king puts God before himself; he turns his back on the usual trappings of earthly kingship: wealth, glory, military might, political allegiances, and temporal comfort.

David's son and successor Solomon started out strong, full of wisdom, and eager to fulfill his father's work, but his reign ended badly due to the usual temptations. What followed was a mixed and motley lot: bad kings, mediocre kings, and a few good kings. But, finally, King Nebuchadnezzar and the Babylonians laid siege to Judah and Jerusalem in 597 B.C., and in 586, the Temple of Solomon was destroyed and most of the people were taken into captivity. The Babylonian Exile lasted about fifty years, ending in 538 when the Persian king, Cyrus the Great, conquered Babylon and allowed the exiled Jews to return home. During that time, the prophet Ezekiel wrote from the foreign land of a future restoration of the Davidic kingdom:

> "MY SERVANT DAVID SHALL BE KING OVER THEM; AND THEY SHALL ALL HAVE ONE SHEPHERD. THEY SHALL FOLLOW MY ORDINANCES AND BE CAREFUL TO OBSERVE MY STATUTES. THEY SHALL DWELL IN THE LAND WHERE YOUR FATHERS DWELT THAT I GAVE TO MY SERVANT JACOB; THEY AND THEIR CHILDREN AND THEIR CHILDREN'S CHILDREN SHALL DWELL THERE FOR EVER; AND DAVID MY SERVANT SHALL BE THEIR PRINCE FOR EVER. I WILL MAKE A COVENANT OF PEACE WITH THEM; IT SHALL BE AN EVERLASTING COVENANT WITH THEM; AND I WILL BLESS THEM AND MULTIPLY THEM, AND WILL SET MY SANCTUARY IN THE MIDST OF THEM FOR EVERMORE. MY DWELLING PLACE SHALL BE WITH THEM; AND I WILL BE THEIR GOD, AND THEY SHALL BE MY PEOPLE" (EZEK. 37:24-27; CF. 34:23-24; HOS. 3:5).

Following their return, the people began to rebuild the temple in Jerusalem. Two facts are noteworthy here: the Jews did not re-establish a kingship, and they did not fall back into the worship of false idols. Things were very difficult, of course, as the people suffered under various foreign rulers, as well as religious leaders who were oftentimes corrupt. Yet they continued to anticipate a time of vindication in which the Davidic kingdom would be restored. The prophet Zechariah, writing just a few years after the return from exile, pointed toward a future time, "the day of the Lord" (Zech. 14:1), when God's rightful kingship would be revealed and recognized throughout the entire world:

> "ON THAT DAY LIVING WATERS SHALL FLOW OUT FROM JERUSALEM, HALF OF THEM TO THE EASTERN SEA AND HALF OF THEM TO THE WESTERN SEA; IT SHALL CONTINUE IN SUMMER AS IN WINTER. AND THE LORD WILL BECOME KING OVER ALL THE EARTH; ON THAT DAY THE LORD WILL BE ONE AND HIS NAME ONE. … THEN EVERY ONE THAT SURVIVES OF ALL THE NATIONS THAT HAVE COME AGAINST JERUSALEM SHALL GO UP YEAR AFTER YEAR TO WORSHIP THE KING, THE LORD OF HOSTS, AND TO KEEP THE FEAST OF BOOTHS" (ZECH. 14:8-9, 16).

And that prophecy brings us to the opening verse of the New Testament: "The book of the genealogy of Jesus Christ, the son of David, the son of Abraham…" (Matt. 1:1).

† THE SON OF DAVID

St. Matthew, in referencing both Abraham and David, purposefully pointed back to two great men who had been promised, through solemn covenants, the heritage of "a great nation," a great name, and a destiny that would bless "all the families of the earth" (Gen. 12:2-3). God also promised an eternal house, kingdom, and throne (2 Sam. 7:16). St. Luke develops this more fully in his opening chapter:

> "IN THE SIXTH MONTH THE ANGEL GABRIEL WAS SENT FROM GOD TO A CITY OF GALILEE NAMED NAZARETH, TO A VIRGIN BETROTHED TO A MAN WHOSE NAME WAS JOSEPH, OF THE HOUSE OF DAVID; AND THE VIRGIN'S NAME WAS MARY. AND HE CAME TO HER AND SAID, 'HAIL, O FAVORED ONE, THE LORD IS WITH YOU!' BUT SHE WAS GREATLY TROUBLED AT THE SAYING, AND CONSIDERED IN HER MIND WHAT SORT OF GREETING THIS MIGHT BE. AND THE ANGEL SAID TO HER, 'DO NOT BE AFRAID, MARY, FOR YOU HAVE FOUND FAVOR WITH GOD. AND BEHOLD, YOU WILL CONCEIVE IN YOUR WOMB AND BEAR A SON, AND YOU SHALL CALL HIS NAME JESUS. HE WILL BE GREAT, AND WILL BE CALLED THE SON OF THE MOST HIGH; AND THE LORD GOD WILL GIVE TO HIM THE THRONE OF HIS FATHER DAVID, AND HE WILL REIGN OVER THE HOUSE OF JACOB FOR EVER; AND OF HIS KINGDOM THERE WILL BE NO END'" (LK. 1:26-33).

The priest Zechariah—the father of Jesus' cousin, John the Baptist—praised God and then prophesied about both John and Jesus:

> "BLESSED BE THE LORD GOD OF ISRAEL, FOR HE HAS VISITED AND REDEEMED HIS PEOPLE, AND HAS RAISED UP A HORN OF SALVATION FOR US IN THE HOUSE OF HIS SERVANT DAVID, AS HE SPOKE

Again, the key elements of kingship are addressed: redemption, salvation, deliverance from enemies and oppression, mercy, and adherence to the covenant. As Bishop Barron notes, David was a true Israelite: he was a singer, that is, "an articulator of the vision of Israel"; he led the people in following and worshipping God; and he was a warrior.

However, the way that Jesus went about establishing his kingdom was a surprise to nearly everyone. In fact, he had to spend quite a bit of time not only proclaiming the kingdom of God, but also explaining it, often through parables. Yet it is hard to deny the centrality of this theme, even though there has been plenty of discussion, even debate, over what the "kingdom of God" is—or is not. Pope Benedict XVI noted in *Jesus of Nazareth: From the Baptism in the Jordan to the Transfiguration* (Doubleday, 2007), the "core content of the Gospels is this: The Kingdom of God is at hand. … This announcement [of the Kingdom] is the actual core of Jesus' words and works. A look at the statistics underscores this. The phrase 'Kingdom of God' occurs 122 times in the New Testament as a whole..." (p. 47). He then observed that there has been a lot of discussion about the relationship between the Church and the kingdom of God. But, he says, that is not the primary issue; the "basic question is actually about the relationship between the Kingdom of God and Christ. It is on this that our understanding of the Church will depend" (p. 49). In short, Benedict makes this crucial observation: "Jesus himself is the Kingdom; the Kingdom is not a thing; it is not a geographical dominion like worldly kingdoms. It is a person; it is he" (p. 49).

The kingdom of God, in other words, is the very presence of God among men. "And the Word became flesh and dwelt among us," wrote the Apostle John, "full of grace and truth; we have beheld his glory, glory as of the only Son from the

Father" (Jn. 1:14). Just as Jesus is the perfect Prophet because he is the actual Word of God, and just as Jesus is the perfect Priest because he is completely holy, divine, and human, Jesus is the perfect King because he is, in his very person, the Kingdom. The kingdom of God, Benedict further explains, "is present whenever [Jesus] is present. ... To pray for the kingdom of God is to say to Jesus: Let us be yours, Lord! Pervade us, live in us; gather scattered humanity in your body, so that in you everything may be subordinated to God and you can then hand over the universe to the Father, in order that 'God may be all in all' (1 Cor. 15:28)" (pp. 146-147).

Jesus began his public ministry by being baptized by John in the desert, away from the city and the temple. He loved his Father's house, but his kingdom has no need for a temple, for he is the Temple. His domain is in the hearts of men; his rule is not reliant on military might or political alliances. As many commentators have pointed out, when Jesus was tempted in the desert, he endured the temptations that the chosen people had given in to while in the desert for forty years (Matt. 4; Lk. 4). But the temptations also echoed those temptations that continually tripped up the kings of Israel and Judah.

The temptation to turn stones into bread was a temptation to provide material comfort for the people while ignoring their deepest eternal need. As Abp. Fulton Sheen affirmed, "There are deeper needs in man than crushed wheat, and there are greater joys than a full stomach" (*Life of Christ* [McGraw-Hill, 1958], 61-62). While many followed Jesus in hopes of being fed, he constantly pointed to the deeper hunger and the everlasting food, for the perfect king desires what it truly best for his people, knowing that man cannot live on bread alone:

> "Jesus answered them, 'Truly, truly, I say to you, you seek me, not because you saw signs, but because you ate your fill of the loaves. Do not labor for the food which perishes, but for the food which endures to eternal life, which the Son of man will give to you; for on him has God the Father set his seal'" (Jn. 26-27).

The second temptation was that of pride, pure and simple. Rather than undergo the Passion and the suffering of the Cross, Satan tempted Jesus to exhibit his power. Rather than humbly follow the will of the Father, Jesus was tempted to go his own way. Rather than demonstrate selfless love, he was tempted to demonstrate self-serving power. This temptation, wrote Sheen, "was to forget the Cross and replace it with an effortless display of power, which would make it easy for everyone to believe in Him" (p. 64).

How many of the Old Testament kings had given into pride and vanity? How many tried to take the quick and easy way, without being true to God or humble before him?

The third temptation was that of temporal power and earthly glory; the only thing required was that Jesus worship Satan. How many of the kings had given into the worship of Baal and other false gods? Even Solomon, when he was old, "turned away his heart after other gods; and his heart was not wholly true to the LORD his God, as was the heart of David his father" (1 Kings 11:4). How many had acquired horses and men instead of relying on God? This temptation would cross Jesus' path again later, when some of the people tried to carry him off and make him a king. Jesus responded by withdrawing to the mountain—that is, he went to pray and commune with the Father (Jn. 6:15). Solomon "did what was evil in the sight of the LORD, and did not wholly follow the LORD, as David his father had done (1 Kings 11:6). Jesus, the son of David, followed the will of the Father perfectly, all the way to the cross.

† THE CROSS & THE KINGDOM

In establishing the Feast of Christ the King, Pope Pius XI reflected on the nature of the kingdom proclaimed by Jesus Christ. In doing so, he began with the Old Testament:

> "The testimony of the Prophets is even more abundant. That of Isaiah is well known: 'For a child is born to us and a son is given to us, and the government is upon his shoulder, and his name shall be called Wonderful, Counselor, God the mighty, the Father of the world to come, the Prince of Peace. His empire shall be multiplied, and there shall be no end of peace. He shall sit upon the throne of David and upon his kingdom; to establish it and strengthen it with judgment and with justice, from henceforth and for ever'" (*Quas Primas,* par. 9).

In turning to the New Testament, Pius XI states:

> "Moreover, Christ himself speaks of his own kingly authority: in his last discourse, speaking of the rewards and punishments that will be

the eternal lot of the just and the damned; in his reply to the Roman magistrate, who asked him publicly whether he were a king or not; after his resurrection, when giving to his Apostles the mission of teaching and baptizing all nations, he took the opportunity to call himself king, confirming the title publicly, and solemnly proclaimed that all power was given him in heaven and on earth. These words can only be taken to indicate the greatness of his power, the infinite extent of his kingdom. What wonder, then, that he whom St. John calls the 'prince of the kings of the earth' appears in the Apostle's vision of the future as he who 'hath on his garment and on his thigh written "King of kings and Lord of lords!".' It is Christ whom the Father 'hath appointed heir of all things'; 'for he must reign until at the end of the world he hath put all his enemies under the feet of God and the Father'" (par. 11).

He later notes that the kingdom established by Jesus "is spiritual and is concerned with spiritual things. Christ by his own action confirms it." Pius XI notes the misunderstandings about this, not only among the Jews in general, but also among the Twelve, whose very selection had been a sign of a new Israel—a new David kingdom. When Pilate asked Jesus, "Are you King of the Jews?" Jesus responded, "My kingship is not of this world; if my kingship were of this world, my servants would fight, that I might not be handed over to the Jews; but my kingship is not from the world" (Jn. 18:33, 36). Note that Jesus did not say that his kingdom was not *in* the world, but was not *of* the world. The kingdom, as St. Augustine wrote about at great length, is the City of God. It is in the world, but its origins are not human while its ends are divine. Pius XI wrote:

> "The gospels present this kingdom as one which men prepare to enter by penance, and cannot actually enter except by faith and by baptism, which, though an external rite, signifies and produces an interior regeneration. This kingdom is opposed to none other than to that of Satan and to the power of darkness. It demands of its subjects a spirit of detachment from riches and earthly things, and a spirit of gentleness. They must hunger and thirst after justice, and more than this, they must deny themselves and carry the cross" (par. 15).

It is the scandal and the paradox of the cross that reveal the kingdom, just as making the sign of the cross reveals those who love and worship the king. The cross is a sign of contradiction; it separates those who sneer, jeer, and revile Jesus from those who behold, embrace, and adore him. Execution on a cross was not only violent and grim, it was a shameful and dishonorable. Yet, as Hans Urs von Balthasar wrote, "His enthronement as King will be complete on the Cross … And so he says, 'Yes,

I am a King.' Not a king within a vanquished world but a King who sits on a throne exalted high above it, exalted by the Cross."

The cross divides mankind because it demands a choice, a judgment about the person of Jesus Christ. But having chosen the cross, the division ends and we are brought into union with the King and his divine life. We receive communion, partaking of his body and blood offered for us on the cross. The cross thus unites Christians, and the inner nature of the kingdom is revealed. As St. Paul wrote to the Colossians, God "has delivered us from the dominion of darkness and transferred us to the kingdom of his beloved Son, in whom we have redemption, the forgiveness of sins. He is the image of the invisible God, the first-born of all creation; for in him all things were created, in heaven and on earth, visible and invisible, whether thrones or dominions or principalities or authorities—all things were created through him and for him. He is before all things, and in him all things hold together" (Col. 1:13-17).

That passage is similar in many ways to the great Christological hymn found in St. Paul's letter to the Philippians, a hymn that highlights how Christ's kingship does not rest on coercion, temporal power, or armies, but is built on perfect humility, service, and self-sacrificial love:

> "Have this mind among yourselves, which is yours in Christ Jesus, who, though he was in the form of God, did not count equality with God a thing to be grasped, but emptied himself, taking the form of a servant, being born in the likeness of men. And being found in human form he humbled himself and became obedient unto death, even death on a cross. Therefore God has highly exalted him and bestowed on him the name which is above every name, that at the name of Jesus every knee should bow, in heaven and on earth and under the earth, and every tongue confess that Jesus Christ is Lord, to the glory of God the Father" (Phil. 2:5-11).

Contrast this to those rulers and kings who tried, with human effort alone, to become gods. The king of Babylon, described by the prophet Isaiah, is a perfect example of this demonic hubris:

> "YOU SAID IN YOUR HEART, 'I WILL ASCEND TO HEAVEN; ABOVE THE STARS OF GOD I WILL
> SET MY THRONE ON HIGH; I WILL SIT ON THE MOUNT OF ASSEMBLY IN THE FAR NORTH; I WILL
> ASCEND ABOVE THE HEIGHTS OF THE CLOUDS, I WILL MAKE MYSELF LIKE THE MOST HIGH.'
> BUT YOU ARE BROUGHT DOWN TO SHEOL, TO THE DEPTHS OF THE PIT." (ISA. 14:13-15; ALSO
> SEE EZEK. 28:2)

All true kingship rests on order and rule and is based on truth, not only on authority. The kingship of God flows from the truth about the nature of the Father, Son, and Holy Spirit. They are perfectly One, yet are three Persons, communing in perfect self-giving love. Those who enter into the kingdom enter into the divine life of the Triune God; they are filled with the power and love of God, able to serve just as the Son of God came to serve. But those who seek their own desires, follow their own passions, and wish to put themselves first will lose the very thing they most need and desire. "But seek first his kingdom and his righteousness," said Jesus, "and all these things shall be yours as well" (Matt. 6:33).

And how does one seek first the kingdom?

> "AND HE SAID TO ALL, 'IF ANY MAN WOULD COME AFTER ME, LET HIM DENY HIMSELF AND TAKE
> UP HIS CROSS DAILY AND FOLLOW ME. FOR WHOEVER WOULD SAVE HIS LIFE WILL LOSE IT; AND
> WHOEVER LOSES HIS LIFE FOR MY SAKE, HE WILL SAVE IT'" (LK. 9:23-24).

The true meaning of Christ's kingship, states the *Catechism*, "is revealed only when he is raised high on the cross" (CCC 440). Yet many reject it. The two criminals crucified with Christ personify the two options available to everyone. Both are sinners; both are able to look directly upon the King. But one sees only a fellow criminal—a target for angry, despairing mockery. The other sees an innocent man; even more, he sees a King: "Jesus, remember me when you come into your kingdom" (Lk. 23:42).

† THE CHURCH & THE KINGDOM

The Church is intimately related to the kingdom; they can be distinguished, but they cannot be separated from one another. The Incarnation is the beginning of the new creation that lives on in the

Church, the Mystical Body of Christ. The Church, as the Second Vatican Council emphasized, is "the initial budding forth" of the kingdom:

> "When Jesus, who had suffered the death of the cross for mankind, had risen, He appeared as the one constituted as Lord, Christ, and eternal Priest, and He poured out on His disciples the Spirit promised by the Father. From this source the Church, equipped with the gifts of its Founder and faithfully guarding His precepts of charity, humility, and self-sacrifice, receives the mission to proclaim and to spread among all peoples the Kingdom of Christ and of God and to be, on earth, the initial budding forth of that kingdom. While it slowly grows, the Church strains toward the completed Kingdom and, with all its strength, hopes and desires to be united in glory with its King" (*Lumen Gentium*, 5).

The *Catechism* teaches that the "Kingdom of God lies ahead of us. It is brought near in the Word incarnate, it is proclaimed throughout the whole Gospel, and it has come in Christ's death and Resurrection. The Kingdom of God has been coming since the Last Supper and, in the Eucharist, it is in our midst. The kingdom will come in glory when Christ hands it over to his Father..." (CCC 2816). The continuity and communion between Christ, the Church, and the Kingdom is essential; it is the heart of God's plan for the unity of mankind:

> "The Church is *ultimately one, holy, catholic,* and *apostolic* in her deepest and ultimate identity, because it is in her that 'the Kingdom of heaven,' the 'Reign of God,' already exists and will be fulfilled at the end of time. The kingdom has come in the person of Christ and grows mysteriously in the hearts of those incorporated into him, until its full eschatological manifestation. Then all those he has redeemed and made 'holy and blameless before him in love,' will be gathered together as the one People of God, the 'Bride of the Lamb,' 'the holy city Jerusalem coming down out of heaven from God, having the glory of God.' For 'the wall of the city had twelve foundations, and on them the twelve names of the *twelve apostles of the Lamb*'" (CCC 865).

In the words of the great Dominican theologian Fr. Aidan Nichols: "The heart of the New Testament proclamation is that through the Son the Father is leading the whole created universe—cosmos and history—to the ultimate fulfillment of the Kingdom" (*Christendom Awake* [Eerdmans, 1999], p. 222). Or, as the *Catechism* states, drawing on *Lumen Gentium*, the Church is "on earth the seed and beginning of that kingdom" (CCC 541-42; 764-5).

To summarize:

• Jesus inaugurated the kingdom of God so man could share in the Father's divine life; the Church is the seed and beginning on earth of that kingdom (CCC 541).

• The coming of the kingdom is brought about through the Paschal mystery of Christ's death and Resurrection (CCC 542).

• The kingdom is growing in the world, in the Church, which is "Jesus' true family" (CCC 764).

• Jesus gave the Church its basic structure, especially by establishing the Twelve and Peter as the head apostle, and "by all his actions, Christ prepares and builds his Church" (CCC 765).

† OUR PARTICIPATION IN CHRIST'S KINGSHIP

The people of God are called to offer everything possible to "the human family" for the sake of that family's salvation and for the kingdom of God (par. 57). Fr. Yves Congar noted, "One is king of what one offers." Because we have been given the Gospel and a share in divine life, we are able to give witness to both, to show how it is Christ who works and lives in us, helping us to be holy and offer spiritual sacrifices (cf. 1 Pet. 2:5). Sister Paula Jean Miller, FSE, in her book *Members of One Body: Prophets, Priests and Kings* (St. Pauls, 1999), writes, "The redemptive nature of the Church's kingly mission, rooted as it is in dominion over self and over all other created realities, more than either of the other offices connotes the moral nature and responsibility of the human person" (p. 160). In other words, the first object of kingly ministry is to attain self-mastery and dominion over all impulses to sin within our own lives. Put another way, we are to pursue, by God's grace, moral purity and exemplary ethical conduct, guided by the teachings of Christ and his Church.

St. John Paul II, in his first encyclical, *Redemptor Hominis* (1979), emphasized this connection:

> "Man's situation in the modern world seems indeed to be far removed from the objective demands of the moral order, from the requirements of justice, and even more of social love. We are dealing here only with that which found expression in the Creator's first message to man at the moment in which he was giving him the earth, to "subdue" it. This first message was confirmed by Christ the Lord in the mystery of the Redemption. This is expressed by the Second Vatican Council in these beautiful chapters of its teaching that concern man's "kingship"; that is to say his call to share in the kingly function—the *munus regale* of Christ himself. The essential meaning of this "kingship" and "dominion" of man over the visible world, which the Creator himself gave man for his task, consists in the priority of ethics over technology, in the primacy of the person over things, and in the superiority of spirit over matter" (par. 16).

He later emphasizes the servant nature of kingship:

> "However, one element seems to stand out in the midst of all these riches: the sharing in Christ's kingly mission, that is to say the fact of rediscovering in oneself and others the special dignity of our vocation that can be described as 'kingship.' This dignity is expressed in readiness to serve, in keeping with the example of Christ, who 'came not to be served but to serve'. If, in the light of this attitude of Christ's, 'being a king' is truly possible only by 'being a servant' then 'being a servant' also demands so much spiritual maturity that it must really be described as 'being a king.' In order to be able to serve others worthily and effectively we must be able to master ourselves, possess the virtues that make this mastery possible. Our sharing in Christ's kingly mission-his 'kingly function' (*munus*) is closely linked with every sphere of both Christian and human morality" (par. 21).

As king, Jesus Christ restored human freedom to its capacity for true dominion, so that by subordinating our bodily passions and personal desires, we can enter completely into self-giving service and charity—reflecting the very nature of the Trinity. However, there are, Sister Miller explains, two major temptations that can thwart or even ruin this essential work:

> "From the beginning, human beings have been faced with a two-pronged temptation: to subject themselves to the created world, which God made for man and woman as the crown of creation, and simultaneously, to refuse to subject themselves to God, and thereby not to acknowledge their creatureliness. The office of kingship requires that man and woman reject both of these options and find the middle way, which alone fulfills the plan of God. This demands, on the one hand, that created persons have dominion over the world and humanize it by means of science, technology, and civilization, and on the other hand, as the created order is perfected, to subject it along with themselves to Christ, who will in turn, subject it together with himself to the Father" (p. 163).

As Sister Miller notes, drawing upon Vatican II and the writings of St. John Paul II, the laity especially fulfill their work of kingship in Christ within the spheres of marriage and family life, the development of culture, socio-economics, public and political service, and international peace. This kingship is closely related to the priesthood shared by all believers, by virtue of baptism, because both are marked by service and are oriented toward the right and true worship of God.

Saint Paul, writing to the Corinthians about the resurrection of the body, explained that Christ is the first fruits from the grave, to be followed at his second coming by those who belong to him. Then comes the end, he says, when Jesus delivers the kingdom to the Father:

> "FOR HE MUST REIGN UNTIL HE HAS PUT ALL HIS ENEMIES UNDER HIS FEET. THE LAST ENEMY TO BE DESTROYED IS DEATH. 'FOR GOD HAS PUT ALL THINGS IN SUBJECTION UNDER HIS FEET.' BUT WHEN IT SAYS, 'ALL THINGS ARE PUT IN SUBJECTION UNDER HIM,' IT IS PLAIN THAT HE IS EXCEPTED WHO PUT ALL THINGS UNDER HIM. WHEN ALL THINGS ARE SUBJECTED TO HIM, THEN THE SON HIMSELF WILL ALSO BE SUBJECTED TO HIM WHO PUT ALL THINGS UNDER HIM, THAT GOD MAY BE EVERYTHING TO EVERY ONE" (1 COR. 15:25-28).

That God may be everything to everyone. That is the goal; that is our purpose; that is the essence of being a human—to be in full and perfect communion with God, who is Love, Life, and Eternal Joy.

Lesson Six: QUESTIONS FOR UNDERSTANDING

Please use the commentary above and the references listed with each question to develop your answers.

1. What do the Evangelists mean when they write of Jesus as "Son of David"? (Matthew 1:1-17; Luke 1:26-33 and 1:68-75; CCC 439, 559)

2. What does Pope Emeritus Benedict XVI mean when he writes in his book *Jesus of Nazareth* that "Jesus himself is the Kingdom..."? (CCC 541-42; 763-66; 2816-21)

3. Pope Pius XI wrote that the kingdom established by Jesus "is spiritual and is concerned with spiritual things." What does that mean regarding the nature of kingdom and the way that it is revealed and known in the world? (Isa. 9:5-6; Jn. 18:36-37; CCC 550, 2816)

4. What is the relationship between the Church and the kingdom? Why is it significant?

5. How do we, especially the laity, share in the kingship of Christ here on earth? (Gen 1:27-30; Matt. 20:25-28; CCC 898, 2013, 2015)

Lesson Six: QUESTIONS FOR APPLICATION

1. What are some words you would use to describe the kingship of Jesus? The kingdom of God? What are some characteristics of Christ as King that you may not have considered or thought about before?

2. In reflecting on Jesus' temptation in the desert, what are the keys to his refutation of Satan's advances? Do you experience temptations toward pride, materialism, and personal glory? How can the example of Christ as humble king and selfless servant be an aid in times of temptation?

. We can sometimes focus so much on the external problems in the Church that we might overlook her supernatural character. Are there problems in the Church—in your local parish or in the Church as a whole—that frustrate you? Can a deeper understanding of the nature of the Church help in coping with those difficulties?

4. If the kingdom of God is, ultimately, the person of Jesus Christ, how can that shape your understanding of your place and work in the kingdom? What are some areas of your life that could benefit from a "kingly" perspective?

BIOGRAPHICAL INFORMATION

MOST REVEREND ROBERT E. BARRON

Bishop Robert Barron is an acclaimed author, speaker, and theologian. He is also the founder of the global media ministry *Word on Fire*, which reaches millions of people by utilizing the tools of new media to draw people into or back to the Catholic Faith. Francis Cardinal George has described him as "one of the Church's best messengers."

Bishop Barron is the creator and host of CATHOLICISM (2011), a groundbreaking, award-winning documentary series about the Catholic Faith. The series has aired on hundreds of PBS stations across the world and has been used by parishes, universities, and schools as an essential resource. Since then, Bishop Barron and Word on Fire also released the follow-up documentary CATHOLICISM: *The New Evangelization* (2013) and are currently wrapping up CATHOLICISM: *The Pivotal Players*, a beautiful new film series on the mystics, scholars, artists, and saints who shaped the Church and changed the world. The series debuted in September 2016 and has been syndicated for national television.

Bishop Barron's website, *WordOnFire.org*, reaches millions of people each year. The site hosts daily blog posts, weekly articles and video commentaries, and an extensive audio archive of homilies. In addition, Bishop Barron also sends out daily email reflections on the Gospel to hundreds of thousands of readers, and episodes of his podcast, *The Word on Fire Show*, have been downloaded by millions.

EWTN (The Eternal Word Television Network) and CatholicTV broadcast Bishop Barron's videos and documentaries to a worldwide audience of over 150 million people. His weekly homilies and podcasts air on multiple radio stations to millions of listeners.

Bishop Barron works with NBC News in New York as an on-air contributor and analyst. He is also a frequent commentator for the *Chicago Tribune*, FOX News, CNN, EWTN, Our Sunday Visitor, the *Catholic Herald* in London, and Catholic News Agency.

He has published numerous essays and articles on theology and the spiritual life, which appear frequently online and in numerous journals. He is a #1 Amazon bestselling author and has published thirteen books.

CARL E. OLSON

Carl E. Olson is the editor of *Catholic World Report* (www.CatholicWorldReport.com) and IgnatiusInsight.com (www.IgnatiusInsight.com), both operated by Ignatius Press. He is the author/co-author of two best-selling books and several hundred articles, essays, columns, and reviews published in a wide range of magazines, newspapers, and websites. Carl wrote the Study Guide for Word On Fire's acclaimed video series, *CATHOLICISM.*

Carl grew up in a Fundamentalist Protestant home and attended Briercrest Bible College, an Evangelical school in Saskatchewan, Canada. He and his wife, Heather, were married in 1994 and entered the Catholic Church together in 1997. Their conversion story appears in the book *Surprised By Truth 3* (Sophia Institute Press, 2002). He earned a master's in Theological Studies from the University of Dallas in 2000. His first book, *Will Catholics Be "Left Behind"? A Catholic Critique of the Rapture and Today's Prophecy Preachers* (Ignatius Press, 2003), was recognized by the Associated Press as one of the best religious titles of the year. Carl Olson is also the co-author, with medievalist Sandra Miesel, of *The Da Vinci Hoax: Exposing the Errors in The Da Vinci Code* (Ignatius Press, 2004). He has written the weekly "Opening the Word" Scripture column for *Our Sunday Visitor* since 2006. He is co-editor, with Fr. David Vincent Meconi, S.J., of the book *Called To Be Children of God: The Catholic Theology of Human Deification* (Ignatius Press).

Carl Olson has been a guest on numerous television and radio programs and networks, including FOX, CNN, BBC, and EWTN, and has spoken at many conferences and parishes. Olson and Heather homeschool their three children in Eugene, Oregon and attend a Byzantine Catholic parish. In his spare time, Olson enjoys recreation with his family, collecting music and books, reading, playing tennis, and scouring used bookstores for hidden treasures.

GLOSSARY

ADVENT: Refers to a specific liturgical season leading up to Christmas, and to the coming of Christ. The word "advent" comes from the Latin word *adventus,* which means "to come to" (see CCC 522-24).

CONDESCENSION: In Catholic theology, the progressive revelation by God of himself, his nature, and his plan of salvation, which respects the limits of man and the need for divine instruction, or pedagogy (see CCC 684, 101, 236).

COVENANT: A solemn agreement between two parties, usually king and subjects or God and humans. In the Old Testament, God established covenants with Noah, Abraham, Moses, and David (see CCC, 56-64). The New Testament—or Covenant—describes the establishment of a new and everlasting covenant through the person, death, and Resurrection of Jesus Christ (CCC, 762, 781; Matt. 26:28; Heb. 8:8-10; 13:20).

DECALOGUE: The Ten Commandments, from the Greek word *dekálogos* (deká=ten; logos=word). The decalogue is recorded in two places in the Pentateuch: Exodus 20:1–17 and Deuteronomy 5:4–21.

DANIÉLOU, JEAN CARDINAL, (1905-74). A French Jesuit theologian, historian, and cardinal noted for his writings on Scripture, patristics, liturgy, and spirituality. At the request of Pope Saint John XXIII, he served as a peritus (expert consultant) to the Second Vatican Council, and he was named a cardinal by Pope Paul VI.

ECCLESIOLOGY: From the Greek word *ekklesia,* from which is derived the word "church" (via the Germanic languages). The theological study of the origin, nature, and mission of the Church.

GUARDINI, ROMANO, (1885–1968). A prominent priest, theologian, professor, and author who was born in Italy but lived most of his life in Germany. He wrote several books on spirituality, prayer, the liturgy, culture, and faith, but is best known for his book, *The Lord,* which is a masterful study of the life of Christ.

HESCHEL, ABRAHAM JOSHUA, (1907-72). A Polish-born American rabbi and a leading twentieth-century Jewish theologian and philosopher. His books include *Man Is Not Alone, God in Search of Man, The Sabbath,* and *The Prophets.*

INCARNATION: The Christian belief that God the Son, the second person of the Trinity, assumed human nature and became man, Jesus Christ, in order to save humanity from sin and death.

MELCHIZEDEK: The king of Salem (Jerusalem), whose name means "my king is righteousness" or "my king is Sedek" (see Gen. 14:18-20; Heb. 7:2), and who met Abraham after Abraham had warred against four kings. Melchizedek, who is identified as a "priest of God Most High," gave Abraham bread and wine, and blessed him. He is mentioned again in Psalm 110:4 and features prominently in the Epistle to the Hebrews, where Jesus is identified as "a high priest forever according to the order of Melchizedek" (Heb. 6:20).

MERTON, THOMAS, (1915-68). A prolific American Catholic writer, poet, and mystic whose best-selling autobiography, *The Seven Storey Mountain* (1948), described his conversion to Catholicism. Merton was a Trappist monk of the Abbey of Gethsemani in Kentucky, and he wrote more than 70 books, including *The Sign of Jonah* and *No Man Is An Island.*

MESSIAH: A title of royalty, derived from a Hebrew word meaning "to anoint." It refers to the Lord's anointed one and was used in the Old Testament primarily in reference to kings, who were anointed as part of the ritual of their installation (cf. 1 Sam. 10:1). By the first century, the term (*Messias* in Greek) was used to refer to a coming Davidic king who would, many Jews believed, save Israel from oppression and re-establish a Davidic kingdom.

PARABLE: A short story, often allegorical in nature but usually drawing upon everyday life and activities, expressing a central moral or theological point. In the Gospels, Jesus uses parables to reveal the kingdom of God to his disciples; fittingly, they usually require authoritative interpretation by Jesus.

PASSOVER: The Jewish celebration, also known in Scripture as the "feast of unleavened bread," which commemorates the liberation, under Moses, of the Hebrews from Egypt (see Exodus 12) after several centuries of slavery by the Pharoahs. The Last Supper, at which Jesus instituted the priesthood, was a Passover meal (Matt. 26; Mk. 14; Lk. 22; Jn. 13, 19).

SACRAMENT: From the Latin word *sacramentum*, meaning "an oath" (itself a translation of the Greek word, *mysterion*), which emphasizes "the visible sign of the hidden reality of salvation" (CCC, par. 774). The *Catechism* states the "sacraments are efficacious signs of grace, instituted by Christ and entrusted to the Church, by which divine life is dispensed to us" (par. 1131).

SATAN: Of Hebrew origin, meaning "adversary" or someone who plots opposition to another. Satan is a fallen heavenly creature who is in complete opposition to God and who seeks to ruin His work. He is also called Beelzebul (Mk. 3:22; Matt 10:25; 12: 24), the evil one (Matt. 13:19; Jn 17:15; 1 Jn. 5:18, 19), the ruler of this world (Jn. 12:31; 14:30), the great dragon (Rev. 12:9), the serpent, or serpent of old (2 Cor. 11:3; Rev 12:9, 14, 14; 20:2), and the tempter (Matt. 4:3; 1 Thess. 3:5). He is also called "the Devil" (Matt. 4:1; 25:41; Lk. 4:2; Jn. 13:2; Acts 10:38), which derives from the Greek word *diabolos* (Latin, diabolus), which also means "slanderer" or "accuser."

SCHMEMANN, ALEXANDER, (1921-1983). An Eastern Orthodox priest, professor, and writer who was one of the most influential Orthodox theologians of the twentieth century. He taught at Saint Vladimir's Orthodox Theological Seminary in New York and wrote several books, including *For the Life of the World: Sacraments and Orthodoxy* and *Church, World, Mission: Reflections on Orthodoxy in the West*.

SHEED, FRANK, (1897-1982). An Australian-born lawyer who was a prominent Catholic speaker, writer, and publisher in the mid-twentieth century. He and his wife, Maisie Ward, founded the Sheed & Ward publishing company, and Sheed authored over twenty books, including *Theology & Sanity, A Map of Life, Theology for Beginners,* and *To Know Christ Jesus*.

SHEEN, ARCHBISHOP FULTON, (1895-1979). Popular American priest, preacher, author, and philosopher. He is considered by many to be the most influential Catholic in twentieth-century America. Millions watched his popular television series, "Life is Worth Living," every week and listened to his radio program, "The Catholic Hour." He wrote dozens of books on numerous topics, including Jesus, Mary, spirituality, politics, philosophy, and marriage.

SHEKHINAH: A Hebrew word that means "the dwelling" or "settling," and refers to the dwelling or settling of the divine presence of God, especially in the Temple in Jerusalem. The word does not appear in the Bible, but the historical and theological background is found in passages including Exodus 25:8 and 40:34, and 1 Kings 8:10.

SOTERIOLOGY: The study of salvation, from the Greek word *soteria*, which means "salvation."

TORAH: The first five books of the Old Testament (Genesis, Exodus, Leviticus, Numbers, Deuteronomy), also called the "five books of Moses" or the Pentateuch. The name comes from the Hebrew word *tôrâ*, meaning instruction or law.